Gyorgy

Gyorgy Nadasdy.

Julia A Pinner

1st Edition

Published in 2016 by

Woodfield Publishing Ltd
Bognor Regis PO21 5EL England
www.woodfieldpublishing.co.uk

Cataloguing in Publication Data is available from the British Library

ISBN 978-1-84683-172-0

Printed and bound in England

Typesetting & page design: Nic Pastorius
Cover design: Klaus Schaffer

Source document:
Gyorgy (final)

Gyorgy

A Teenage Hungarian Freedom Fighter's Story

GYORGY NADASDY
& JULIA PINNER

Woodfield Publishing Ltd

Bognor Regis ~ West Sussex ~ England ~ PO21 5EL

tel 01243 821234 ~ **e/m** info@woodfieldpublishing.co.uk

Interesting and informative books on a variety of subjects

For full details of all our published titles, visit our website at
www.woodfieldpublishing.co.uk

For my wife Sylvia, daughters Luci and Laura, granddaughters Emmie and Elba, my family in Britain whom I love dearly; to my sister Nusi, brother Peter, and to the memory of my mother and brothers Pali and Pisti, my Hungarian family.

English people took in the Hungarians in 1957 and settled us in with love and support: we were welcomed and we cannot thank them enough.

This book is dedicated to the memory of the Freedom Fighters and all those who lost their lives, including the grieving families.

Photograph of Gyorgy entitled 'A fourteen-year-old Freedom Fighter'
from page 112 of *A Brave Nation* by Anna Ambrosy (*source unknown*).

Contents

Gyorgy looking bewildered in a rubble-strewn Budapest street.
Source: Life History, Time.com. (*Photo:* Michael Rougier)

Acknowledgements

I want to thank my wife Sylvia, brother Peter and sister Nusi for their support, Anna Kasmani who helped in Austria, Julia Pinner Cert.Ed. who wrote the story, researched and referenced it, and Dr. Jane Bownas MSc, MA, PhD whose help was invaluable.

Gyorgy is best man at
the wedding of John
Pinner and Julia Perry
at Tamworth
Methodist Church,
Victoria Road on 30th
March 1968.

Just married.
Julia and John
outside the
church.

Preface

I have known Sylvia and Gyorgy Nadasdy since I was twenty years old. They introduced me to my future husband John Pinner in 1967 and we have kept in touch ever since.

When Gyorgy's brother Peter saw photographs of Gyorgy in books about the Hungarian Uprising he sent them to Gyorgy from Australia, and this inspired Gyorgy to tell his own story. Gyorgy showed the books to my husband John and I and we were fascinated to see the photographs of him taken by press reporters at the time, one of which adorns the front cover of this book.

Because I love history and knew little about this short, tragic episode in the long and eventful history of Hungary, I offered to write down Gyorgy's story.

In common with thousands of other freedom fighters, Gyorgy was forced to flee his native country to escape the revenge of the Communist regime after the failure of the uprising.

Many countries, including the United Kingdom, enthusiastically offered asylum to the Hungarian refugees – and that is how Gyorgy, at the age of 14, came to live in our hometown of Tamworth in Staffordshire to start his new life in England. That was 60 years ago and Gyorgy has lived here ever since, marrying and raising a lovely family.

As I write this, in 2016, the subject of refugees is very much in the news so it is perhaps fitting to remember another time when thousands of people were left stranded by circumstances beyond their control but governments and ordinary citizens all over the world rallied to their aid, not least the people of Great Britain. Back then everyone agreed that it was our moral duty to do whatever we could to help – and Gyorgy and his family remain forever grateful that he was given the opportunity to start a new life in a free country. But, as you will read, it was by no means 'a bed of roses' and he worked very hard for many long years to earn a living and eventually obtain British citizenship.

His story is an inspiring one and deserves to be told and I am delighted to have been given the opportunity to help him tell it.

Julia Pinner
Tamworth, August 2016

Gyorgy's mother, Anna Papai, looking like a film star.

Gyorgy's father, Gyorgy Wranyecz, Head Chef at Hotel Gundel, Budapest, with some of his culinary creations.

Introduction

Gyorgy Nadasdy was born in Budapest in 1942 and the events of October 1956, when he was just fourteen years of age, changed his life dramatically when, together with his brother Peter, he became a Freedom Fighter and later a refugee.

Hungarians lived through hell during two weeks of a Revolution that shook the world. In Gyorgy's own words:

"The reason that I wanted to write this book is to tell the story about the Freedom Fighters from a fourteen year olds point of view and about my life before and after those events. When the fighting was all over, we realized that Hungary was the only country to get involved with trying to stamp out communism, and to fight against the Russians. Therefore my congratulations go to the Hungarians who put their lives at risk by fighting against communism and the Soviet regime.

I am really grateful to the British people for helping us Hungarians to settle here and give us a better life. I cannot thank them enough for accepting us here in 1957."

Gyorgy's story is set out in the following chapters, with the exception of Chapters 8-10 in which I needed to diverge from Gyorgy's own words, as at that time he was totally unaware of events such as Hungary's radio pleas for help, international casualties and the Lord Mayor of London's "Hungarian Aid Appeal."

I added this introduction to provide a short background to the events described in Gyorgy and Peter's chapters about the Uprising.

At the end of World War 2, Soviet troops had liberated Hungary from occupation and established a Communist regime. These troops remained in the country and their removal was one of the main demands made by Hungarian students at the start of the Uprising. They wanted their sixteen demands to be heard over the radio station in Budapest, which was the nerve centre of the communist regime in Hungary (see Appendix 1 & 2.)

Gyorgy's eldest brother, Peter, who had left Hungary in November 1956 and emigrated to Australia, sent Gyorgy a booklet in the late 1980s which outlined the reasons for and the nature of the Uprising (Appendix 3). Three out of five writers quoted in this booklet were Australian leaders: E. Gorman, K. Shann and Dr. R. Walker, who were requested by the United Nations, at the time of the revolt and afterwards, to write objectively about it. Not one of the five was given permission by the Communist regime to visit Hungary. Instead they collected evidence from other governments and witnesses – 111 in all – representing all levels of Hungarian society. Their testimonies filled 2,000 pages.

Julia Pinner, August 2016

Passers by read the list of student demands pinned on a tree in Rakoczi Boulevard (on the corner by the University and Museum) published in a special issue of *Jovo Mernokei* (*Engineers of the Future*) the student journal from the Technical University, 2,000 copies of which were printed. (Source MTI/Tamas Fenyes.)

University students carry flags as they demonstrate on the Danube bank, Budapest on 23rd October 1956, the day on which the uprising against Soviet communist rule broke out in Hungary. The state coat of arms, made in the Soviet model, has been cut from the centre of the flag. (Photo: MTI/Tamas Munk)

The Hungarian Revolution

Timeline[1]

Pre-Uprising: Russian control of the economy had made the people poor; there was no freedom, schools were told what they could teach and the communists had banned religion, with some churches being pulled down. The secret police made all Hungarians afraid. They were known as the AVO (Államvédelmi Osztálya) [State Protection Department] until 1956, when the government changed their name to the AVH (Államvédelmi Hatóság) [State Protection Authority] in an attempt to make them sound less intimidating. Nevertheless, they were hated by most Hungarians, who were desperate for major changes.

The battle for Budapest, which began on October 23rd 1956 happened in three phases: the first was the initial Uprising, which appeared to be successful and ended on October 29th when the Russians withdrew from Budapest. The second phase was brief but sweet. For five days Budapest delighted in the mistaken belief that Hungary was at last free of Russian domination and the AVH. The third phase began on November 4th when Russian tanks and troops stormed back into the city in huge numbers, crushing the revolution.

23rd October 1956: About 200,000 citizens took to the streets of Budapest (illegally,

according to communist rule) demanding independence and the withdrawal of Soviet troops. Word had been spread the night before via leaflets distributed throughout the city by students, stating their sixteen demands, which the people supported enthusiastically. Most of the crowd joined demonstrators outside the parliament building where, by 6pm, 200-300,000 people were gathered. In the evening the AVH secret police guarding the building which housed the Radio Station, where the students hoped to have their demands broadcast, threw tear gas bombs from the upper windows and fired the first shots into the crowd.

These first shots marked the start of a hard-fought five-day battle between the protesters and Soviet armoured vehicles and the AVH. The peaceful demonstration of young people, students, factory workers and others had become a violent uprising. Ambulances with Red Cross insignia arrived, but instead of first aid teams, members of the AVH police emerged, wearing doctors' coats and white caps. Members of the infuriated crowd attacked them, enabling the demonstrators to seize their first weapons. Hungarian soldiers sided with the crowd. Workers from surrounding districts learnt of the situation by telephone, seized trucks and drove into Budapest. The statue of Stalin which stood in a park at the centre of the city was pulled down and smashed to pieces.

---

[1] Information for this section has been gathered from: www.gcsehistory.org.uk and A Brave Nation by Anna Ambrosy, pages 93-95

24th October 1956: Rioting took place throughout Budapest. Imre Nagy, a moderate and a westerner, was reinstated as Prime Minister: his government included non-communist members, ending the one party state in Hungary, which showed that he was aware of the wishes of the people. He was faced with a country in turmoil. He wanted to create a multi-party independent state. Nagy requested that Khruschev withdraw Soviet troops from Hungary, which was agreed. Nagy announced that Hungary would withdraw from the Warsaw Pact and become a neutral, social democracy.

Workers heard of the situation by telephone and radio, seized trucks, gathered arms and drove to Budapest. Freedom fighters were workers – even children as young as 12 – and students who fought in small groups, armed with a few obsolete guns and any other weapons they could obtain. "Molotov Cocktails" (petrol-filled bottles with a flaming cloth wick inserted in the neck, which exploded on impact) were frequently and successfully used.

25th October: Soviet Tanks guarding the Parliament Building opened fire on unarmed protesters in Pest, killing many in a massacre that shocked the nation.

26th October: Unrest spread to the countryside. Prime Minister Nagy again called for withdrawal of Soviet Troops.

27th October: Mr Nagy formed a government of Communist and non-Communist members.

28th October: The start of five days of freedom. Mr Nagy made a broadcast promising widespread reform. A ceasefire was ordered. Nagy stated that he would disband the AVH. Negotiations would start with the USSR for the immediate withdrawal of Soviet forces. The Austrian Foreign Ministry sent the following message to London, Paris and Washington:

"To all appearances, the uprising in Hungary will come to an end following massive Soviet military intervention. In that event, it can be presumed that larger Hungarian armed formations will cross into Austria."

30th October: Soviet troops withdrew from Hungary. There was freedom of speech and freedom of religion. The Catholic leader of Hungary, Cardinal Mindszenty, head of the Catholic Church, was released from prison. The ceasefire became fully effective. Many buildings lay in ruins but no looting took place. The people began to clear the rubble and get back to normal. The people released political prisoners detained and tortured by the Soviet regime.

1st November: The Hungarian Government announced its intention to leave the Warsaw Pact. Soviet troops re-entered Hungary. Freedom fighters agreed to be amalgamated into the National Guard. Mr Nagy asked the United Nations to defend Hungary's neutrality. International reaction and response to the Hungarian Revolution was relatively muted as it occurred at the same time as the Suez Crisis, involving Western powers with conflict in Egypt.

Giving help risked a war starting and both sides in the Cold War now had nuclear powers. The Suez Crisis was considered more important and of greater relevance to the West than the suffering of the Hungarians, so Britain, France and America condemned the Soviets but took no action other than to provide funds for refugee camps in Austria and offer to accept large numbers of refugees, along with many other countries.

3rd November: Soviet armoured forces congregated on the border while negotiations continued to have them withdraw. But before an agreement was reached, about 3,500 Soviet tanks and 1,000 supporting vehicles had poured into the country, in battle formation. The Hungarian Army, the National Guard and groups of freedom fighters, equipped with light weapons, fought side by side against advancing tanks.

4th November: *The Russian Terror* started at 4am that Sunday. Mr Nagy made a final appeal by radio to the West for help at 5.15am that morning. Approximately 1,000 Soviet tanks entered Budapest and started to shoot at every centre of resistance, which had defied them during the first battle for freedom in October. The Russian soldiers had one order: shoot! Terror prevailed across Budapest when anything that moved was shot – even a woman carrying bread. Orders were, if one shot came from a house, destroy the whole house. If there were many shots from a street, shoot down every building in the street.

Buildings were pulverised and thousands of Hungarians buried alive. Women in queues were shot, even ambulances and Red Cross workers were mercilessly shot down. Nurses attending the wounded were executed at point blank range. Freedom fighters were trapped in various barracks, public buildings and blocks of flats. The Russians intended to kill them to the last man, which they knew, so they fought on bravely till death claimed them. By this day, Soviet armoured units were in control of the Danube bridges, the parliament Building and the central telephone exchange. Mr Nagy was arrested.

The United Nations called for a Soviet withdrawal. An appeal was made at 8am by Budapest Radio to the world to assist the people of Hungary, and then radio silence. The last words heard were "Help! Help! Help!"

5th November: Local resistance continued until this time, when most of the freedom fighters ran out of ammunition. Also, the fighting groups knew that further battles would mean the annihilation of the capital, so they stopped fighting. The Soviet armed forces caused considerable loss of life and heavy destruction in an unremitting onslaught in Budapest. This was the second intervention; the fiercest fighting took place in working class suburbs such as Corvin Lane, Ujpest and Csepepel Island and Sztalinvaros (now Dunapentele) the important industrial centre. Factory workers, Hungarian officers and local garrison men fought together.

7th November: Mr Janos Kadar (previously First Secretary of the Central Committee of the party) formed a new government. It was a 'puppet' government to reflect the wishes of Moscow. Soviet control was re-established. Reforms that Nagy had implemented were quickly repealed.

From 7th – 14th November Austria was swamped with refugees; seven nations offered help.

11th November: The Soviets claimed victory over the revolutionaries. There was a passive resistance to Soviet rule by the workers, who opted to strike on 11th and 12th December. (Factories had been closed for two months now.) The Russians resorted to mass arrests. Thousands of captives were crowded onto trains or in trucks and deported to the USSR; many did not return. The death penalty was instituted for many offence's including strikes. Nagy sought refuge in the Yugoslav embassy.

A great terror followed the crushing of the revolution. Hundreds of people were sentenced to death while others received long and short-term prison sentences, or were transported to perpetual slavery.

In addition, about 200,000 refugees left Hungary, with a detrimental effect on the already decimated population.

20th December: A State Information Office was opened to control the press. The Revolutionary Council of Intellectuals and the Writer's Union were dissolved.

By 1957 non-Communist organisations had been excluded from appearing in any role in public life.

January 1957: TIME magazine made 'the Hungarian Freedom Fighter' its *Man of the Year*.

Early 1957: The purge continued. Revolutionaries known as the "Enemy of the People" involved in the uprising were sought out and deported to slavery, imprisoned in overcrowded cells or executed. This process continued until 1962.

September 1957: United Nations Report on *The Problem of Hungary* published (see Appendix 4). *Conclusion*: What took place in Hungary in October and November 1956 was a spontaneous national uprising in reaction to long-standing grievances, which had caused resentment among the people.

17th June 1958: Radio Budapest announced that Imre Nagy and other leaders of the freedom fighters would be hanged. Their death sentences were soon carried out, despite promises from Janos Kadar that no punitive action would be used against the freedom fighters.

My Early Years in Budapest

I WAS BORN ON 17th September 1942 in Budapest, the Hungarian capital city, which is split into two halves, Buda and Pest, on either side of the River Danube. We lived in Pest, the flatter part of the city, in a tenement on Dembisky Utca (Road) in District VII. Our block (Block 6), had 3 levels and we lived on the first floor in flat 15b. We had one living room (in which all six of us also slept), a kitchen with only a cold tap (where we also washed ourselves) and an old-fashioned wood-burner stove (we used coal as well sometimes, when Mum could afford it) to heat the place and to cook on, plus a small pantry. There was no toilet inside the flat; you had to go outside to one that was shared by all the other residents, quite a few of them, as there were 12-14 apartments to each floor with just one toilet on each level, with a wooden seat and a hole beneath it!

My father, Gyorgy Wranyecz, was said to be one of the best chefs in Europe and worked at the Hotel Gundel in Budapest before and after the Second World War. My mother, Anna Papai, also worked there as a kitchen maid.

The Gundel was (and still is) a famous establishment offering fine dining to a wealthy clientele. It is located in the *Varosliget* (City Park) in District XIV, near to the City Zoo.

Further proof of my father's skills as a chef come from the fact that his name appears on the frontispiece of a book called *Lexikon der Kuche* by Richard Hering, first published in 1907 in Hungarian, English, French and German (see below). It looks as if Dad added to a later edition. It is not a recipe book but a lexicon of cookery terms for professionals. It is still in print today.

My sister Nusi told me that Dad was also a Chef in France at one time, although I don't know much about this; my sister is 12 years older than me and remembers earlier years.

The Communist Hungarians – the better off ones – used the Gundel in postwar years after the Russians had 'liberated' countries such as Austria, Poland, Czechoslovakia, Romania and Hungary from German occupation. Unfortunately, the Russians remained in Hungary and we all came under Soviet rule.

Gyorgy's father worked in the heart of Varosliget (City Park). Inaugurated in 1894, the Gundel is now a high class restaurant which has been visited by many VIPs including HM Queen Elizabeth II and His Holiness Pope John Paul II.

The Hotel Gundel first opened in 1894 and employed only the finest chefs. It gained a reputation for excellent quality and later served such dignitaries as Her Majesty Queen Elizabeth II and His Holiness Pope John Paul II.

My older sister Nusi was born in 1930 and my older brother Peter in 1940. I also had two younger brothers: Pisti (born in 1953) and Pali (born in 1944), both of whom sadly died a few years ago.

When I was a child I suppose that we were a middle/working class family. I cannot remember much about growing up during the war , except that we spent a lot of time in the cellars beneath the apartment block, which served as air raid shelters. I got on well with my sister Nusi; we were close and she was like another mum to me.

I spent a lot of time with her when she visited Grandma and also at her house after she was married. I often ran to her when I

needed help, as Mum was always working, so we children had to look after ourselves and each other for much of the time.

Budapest was very much like London during World War Two. There were lots of Blitzes in 1944 and we had an addition to the family during this year, my brother Pali. During the wartime years there was nothing much available and there were many shortages, so we had to make do with what we had. Clothes were passed down from brother to brother. We didn't have socks, so we wrapped our feet in rags or whatever we had to keep them warm from October to February, when temperatures dropped well below freezing. Most people also put newspaper soles into their boots to help keep warm. Not the communists, though; they had money!

My sister was sent to stay with our grandmother in a little village away from the city. I remember going there myself when I was about three years old. There

The main entrance to the apartment block where Gyorgy and his family lived on Dembisky Utca (Road) in District VII in Pest

The view from inside the block, showing the courtyard and three levels. Gyorgy's family lived on the 1st level, Block 6, flat 15b.

The Animal Hospital in Budapest, near to where Gyorgy lived (photo taken in 2015).

Varosliget (City Park), where Gyorgy often played and not far from where he lived. (Taken in 2015).

weren't any roads, just dirt tracks and we walked everywhere or used a horse and cart; mostly we walked. In the villages it was normal for women to wash clothes in streams; times were hard. My sister was looking after grandmother, who was very sick. I can remember watching Nusi washing Grandma down at night, lifting her into bed and then looking after us all. At that time she was only fifteen years old. When the war was over we went back to live with my parents in Budapest, although we didn't see much of them because they were always out at work.

Public phone boxes didn't take currency – you had to buy a token to use the phone. There weren't any phones in houses in those days. We would go outside to play in the park and search the phone boxes in case any tokens had been left behind. We could swap the tokens for money, which we usually gave to Mum, although we sometimes bought sweets for ourselves!

We lived with a curfew after 1945, when the country was under Russian rule. We children had to be off the streets and back home by 7pm, after which time we were only allowed out of our houses for an officially permitted reason, and had to be accompanied by our parents. There wasn't any freedom and people's lives were controlled by the state.

Our apartment block housed 36 families and had a caretaker, who locked the doors at 11pm. Nobody had their own key for the main door, you had to ring the bell to be let in and had to have a very good reason for staying out after curfew. If the caretaker didn't believe your reason for being late he would phone the police, who would then question you further as to where you had been. Since Dad often worked late at the Gundel he couldn't be back in time for

curfew, but the caretaker knew this, so it was allowed.

Another memory is of a coal merchant who lived in our block and stored coal in the cellar. During school holidays my older brother Peter and I used to help him shovelling the coal into sacks, ready to sell. We earned a little pocket money for doing this, which we gave to Mum, as Dad had died by this time. She worked day and night and didn't have much rest. Later I became a coalman in Britain and wonder if this is where the idea came from!

When we were let out of the flat we used to go wild, playing in the street. None of us had any toys but we could make rough balls for a game of cricket and use sticks as a bat – or use a shirt rolled up as a football. My brother Peter would not play with us; he preferred his own mates, who were two or three years older than me. Pali was my younger brother and I had to look after him. He often got me into trouble when he ran home crying. Mum always blamed me... so out came Dad's belt and I got a good hiding!

In 1947 I started school. We always walked there and back; there wasn't a bus service. On the first day I cried because I did not want to go and when my mother left me there I was afraid she would not come back. After all, whenever I was naughty she used to say she would give me away to the gypsies! After a few days I settled down and started to make friends but at the back of my mind I was still afraid that one day nobody would come to collect me, so my first years at school were not very happy.

I remember that one day Mum and Dad locked me in the flat and took both of my brothers out with them. I cried because I was angry that I was left alone and I was probably scared. I opened the window with the intention of jumping out but it was too far to jump; the flat was on the first floor. I could see the roof of a small building below so, in a temper, I collected all the knives, forks, spoons and saucepans I could find and, one by one, threw them onto the roof below!

When my parents came home I was very silent, so they knew that I had done something wrong. It didn't take long for them to discover what it was. When my mother set about the task of preparing some food she opened the cupboards; no saucepans! She opened the drawers; no utensils! Mum and Dad started arguing. He must have had a few beers. He got hold of me, shouting and shaking me, asking what I had done with them. Peter and Pali ran to the window because they were scared and saw what was on the roof below.

"Oh my God! What have you done?" Mum wailed.

Dad gave me a good belting. The next day I was black and blue. I will always remember that day.

It was not many months later that my Dad came home as drunk as a Lord. He started shouting at my mother and hitting her; he picked up plates and smashed them against the wall. We all gathered around Mum so that he wouldn't hit her again.

When he wasn't drinking Dad was a different man altogether. I realise now that he was under a lot of stress because of the times. In a way we all liked him. The Gundel Hotel where he worked was near the City Park, not far from our flat in Pest and sometimes he would take us to work with him. We would be left to play in the back garden of the hotel and these were days that we liked. When he had a moment to spare

he would come outside to see us and give us bits of food and drink. Sadly, I did not get to know him all that well.

During 1949 he became ill and was at home, bed-ridden. We noticed that he was always coughing. We all lived in the same room; Mum and three of us in the double bed and Dad in a makeshift bed. A week later he went to hospital and never came out. Two days later he died of pulmonary thrombosis; he had needed penicillin but it was new at that time and only those who could afford it could have it, but we were poor.

After Mum had buried Dad, the hard times really came. She worked day and night to make ends meet. Each morning she would get us up to send us school, then she would go cleaning for a local couple who owned a greengrocers shop. They were pretty good to Mum; although they paid her very little money, they gave her any fruit that was bruised or just starting to go bad. She used to cut out the bad bits so at least we could all have fruit such as apples and pears to eat. We also had lemons, which in were used in tea (Hungarians don't add milk to tea; just sugar and lemon) but I didn't see oranges or bananas until I went to Austria, years later.

Mum used to catch a little sleep in the afternoons and then at night she went off to clean offices until morning. She would salvage any food left behind to be disposed of by the office workers in the daytime and bring it home to supplement the diet of her four children.

Sometimes there was only dry bread left in the bottom of the wardrobe where she kept the food. Mum used to save this to make breadcrumbs to have with chicken on Sundays. That's the only time she could afford it. She used to make chicken soup out of the liver, heart, head and feet of the chicken, which she always got cheaply. We also ate tripe, offal and pig's feet. I don't remember ever having cheese and we ate eggs only occasionally.

Mum often made simple dishes with any old potatoes, carrots and parsnips that she could afford. Nothing was ever thrown away. There wasn't a fridge so food was put on the cold floor or windowsill and used up the next day. Times were very hard for her but she was like a Saint.

I remember the first Christmas in 1949, after my Dad passed away, when I was seven years old. That Christmas we all had a present. I had a wooden lorry (perhaps that was why I became a lorry driver!) For about another three years I was given a wooden lorry each Christmas, every year slightly different. Much later I realised it was the *same* lorry, painted different colours each year!

When I was older I started to make friends with the rest of the kids in the flats and neighbouring houses. We used to play in the street outside the apartment. Opposite us was a Veterinary Hospital and School surrounded by parkland, so we used to go and play in this park. The trouble was that it was forbidden to enter those premises, so whenever we did, we would be chased by the caretakers and the police! It was great fun and we always got away because we knew where the holes in the fences were and where the bent railings left a gap big enough for us to squeeze through but too small for them!

The apartment houses were numbered. I lived in block six and another pal lived in block four. In each block there were about 40 families. We used to have street fights against the kids who lived in blocks eight and ten. Luckily for us there were fewer families living these blocks, so we outnumbered them! Sometimes our battles used to get out of hand and we would end up throwing stones and bottles.

I made friends with my older brother Peter's mates but in doing so I fell in with the wrong crowd and started playing truant from school. We used to go to the park or over the River Danube to Buda, where the mountains were. We didn't have any money, so we would ride on the couplings at the back of trams, where the conductor could not see us. We were not put off by how dangerous it was, although we knew that some kids had fallen off, lost a leg or an arm or even been killed.

Playing in the mountains there were many other dangers. Apart from the natural hazards there were live rounds of ammunition and bombs scattered about, left over from the Second World War. We used to collect them or even try exploding them! Cleaning up after the war was very inadequate – even nowadays old munitions are still being found.

On autumn days we used to go scrumping in the local park, where there were orchards of cherries, apples, peaches, pears and other fruits. Sometimes we were caught and given a good hiding by the Park Keeper. Other times we ended up at the Police Station in Buda. Mum could not collect me from there, so the police used to take me and other kids from Pest back across the Danube. We were put into a police cell with older men and women and maybe given a bit of dry bread and a drink of water, not that this bothered me much; sometimes it was more than we had at home.

The Soda Siphon

AT THE AGE of seven I stole an empty soda siphon in order to get the deposit money, which I intended to give to my mum to help her look after us all. But I was caught and as a result I was sentenced to attend a Reform School (similar to a British Approved School) for seven years.

I remember my sister taking me to the station and putting me on a train that would take me to the school, situated in a village far from the city. I cried my eyes out. I was only seven. How could a punishment so harsh have been dispensed for such a minor crime? Even now I cannot understand it.

The school was in a large house where we boarded, ate, slept and learned. There were five or six rooms with about ten to fifteen kids sleeping in each one. The 'boss' of each room was an older boy. These bullies were put in charge to keep order and received better treatment as a reward. Their tactics were pretty crude. For example they might tell a couple of the younger boys to start hitting each other in the face. The first to cry was the weakest and had to do the dirty work for a week.

We were out of bed at six o'clock each morning. Before we started our lessons we had to go to the playing field to run around, in winter and summer. The summer wasn't too bad but in winter it could be minus 20 degrees and we were only in our games shorts, running around for 30 minutes. It certainly toughened us up; we were always

fit. After that we had a meagre breakfast before starting our lessons.

These lessons were conducted under a very strict dictatorship; if we stepped out of line there was trouble. We were taught to read and write Hungarian but were also obliged to learn Russian. History was also taught, but only from communist perspective. Communist propaganda was constantly drilled into us; we were forced to breathe, eat and sleep Communism.

There was one good teacher who used to tell us stories about the good things in life before we went to sleep. I think he may have had kids of his own and felt sorry for us.

We weren't allowed to wander around outside; this was a prison-type institution with bars at the windows. If we went anywhere it was for government work, such as fruit picking in the summer for local farmers. We didn't get paid, we just had a few bits of fruit. In winter we would go wool picking in the fields nearby, scavenging for tufts of wool that had become snagged on thorns or barbed wire. We were freezing cold, as there were no overcoats for us, just ordinary clothes with feet wrapped in rags. We were also taught by local farmers how to plough in a perfectly straight line with a horse-drawn plough. There were no tractors.

During every Communist holiday and especially on 1st May there were big parades in the park in Budapest in front of Stalin's statue. The teachers made us schoolchildren stand to attention like soldiers for a long time in the heat. Some kids used to faint.

When I was about 11 years old and still at Reform School we learned how to make gas bombs, ammunition and air raid shelters, together with how to give people first aid, in case there was another World War. Everyone was expected to be ready in case it happened again.

The food was basic and we had the same meals every week. I remember feeling hungry but we must have had sufficient because we always had enough energy to do games and work outside, even in very cold weather. We suffered from occasional coughs and colds but no medicines were available; we just had to wait for the symptoms to wear off.

While I was at Reform School my mother had a baby boy, who she named Pisti, born in 1953. The story is this. In the flats where we lived there was a basement where a lady had a cobbler's business. She had a clever man working for her called Pisti Nadasdy, who made shoes, boots and sandals, all by hand. He lived on the first floor with a lady but they used to argue a lot and eventually she kicked him out and he had nowhere to live. The business lady who this man worked for was Godmother to my younger brother Pali, who was born in 1944, so she asked my mum a favour, to take Pisti in. Mum agreed and made friends with him. He used to give us a little money to get sweets. I cannot remember him very well as I was still at school and didn't live there; but he was all right.

They weren't married but the relationship blossomed and in 1953 there was an addition to the family, Pisti junior, whom we all liked because he was a good little boy. I did not see him very much due to being in the Reform School but when I was at home during the brief two-week summer holiday I was allowed, I would take him out to the park with me, which wasn't far from where we lived. He used to love it; half way home he would fall asleep, so I carried him on my back until we got home, then washed and fed him, before putting him to bed. I was very much the big brother as I was 11 years old when he was born.

I stayed at the same school for three years (7-10 years) after which I was sent to another similar establishment for three more years (aged 10-13) which fortunately was not as bad as the first one. There were some Greek families living there (I think they worked there) and their children were also there. There were some other Greek children there but I don't know why they were there. I made friends with a boy called Delkosz Jorgosz, who was the same age as me and who taught me a little Greek. Unfortunately, this place also had bullies and we both used to get picked on.

By the time I was 13 years old, in 1955, the authorities sent us to another detention school in Budapest; the third and final one for me. Delkosz came with me to this school.

At last, in June 1956, I finally went home to live with my family, who I had seen for only two weeks a year for the past seven years. When I arrived there were no emotions, no kissing or cuddling. Life was still hard and we all just had to get on with it.

And that was the end of my seven-year separation from my family – all for the theft of an empty soda siphon to get a few extra pence for my mother!

My Part in The Uprising

I STARTED WORK IN early October 1956 as an apprentice for a bus building company called Ikarus. I was given a small work booklet that showed my work number, name, date of birth and the date that I started work. It showed that I had started an apprenticeship with the company and was signed by the boss. It was supposed to be changed after one year and signed each month, but that didn't happen because the Uprising started just two weeks after I had been taken on at Ikarus.

At the time I didn't know any details regarding how the uprising had started. We didn't have a radio or television at home or purchase a daily newspaper like people do in Britain. Besides, the Hungarian Communist Party was in control of the media and wouldn't allow anything to be published which was critical of the regime. So when the uprising started I, along with most of the other ordinary citizens in Budapest, didn't know much about it. The way we found out was by word-of-mouth from people in the street.

At 14 years of age much of the politics was over my head but I certainly knew about the secret police (AVH) and their methods of terror and had first-hand experience of the harshness of the communist regime, having been subjected to it for seven years whilst in reform school. All I knew was that if there was going to be an uprising, I wanted to be part of it.

It soon emerged that the main demand of the protesters was that Russian troops be withdrawn from Hungary. No Hungarian was going to argue with that. We were all fed up with the Communists and their rules and the secret police.

The statue of Stalin which stood in a nearby park became the first focus for the People's anger. I went into the park with Delkosz and others to find out what was going on. We only lived a couple of miles away from the park, so got there quickly. By the time we arrived there were thousands of people gathered around the statue, calling for it to be destroyed. We stayed there until it came down. At the time I didn't realise that my brother Peter had been involved. There were too many people gathered around for me to get a clear view.

After the statue was toppled there were rumours circulating among the crowd that fighting was taking place in various parts of the city. Delkosz and I followed a group of older people out of the park and went to find out what was happening in the area round Corvin ter.

In the days that followed Delkosz and I went wherever we dared. I had a rifle and ammunition and Delkosz had a handgun as well as a rifle. We used to change our hats and jackets so that no one would recognise us. The Freedom Fighters would help each other to hide. Sometimes we hid in cellars

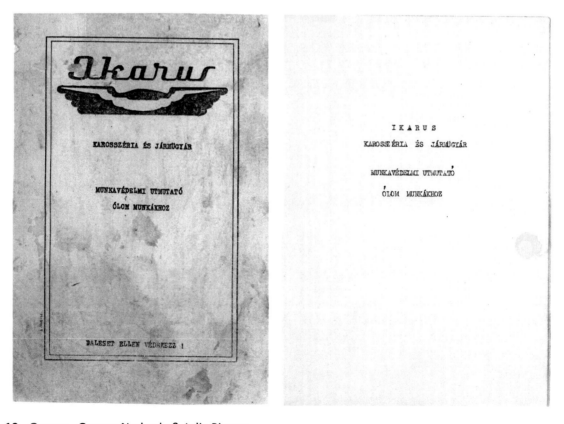

Gyorgy's identity book, dated 4th October by Ikarus Bus Company, where he worked briefly in 1956.

Pages from the Ikarus rule book.

when we heard that the Russians were nearby, and we also needed to hide our guns in case we were found.

We weren't frightened even though we knew that we were very much outnumbered. Mum didn't know that I had become a Freedom Fighter and I didn't go home during this period; she must have been worried. Delkosz and I slept alongside other fighters in cellars or wherever we could hide. We wandered around the streets where the trouble was taking place. We fed on whatever we could get, mostly given to us by Hungarian supporters. We stayed in Pest all the time and didn't cross the River Danube.

Soon there were photographers from newspapers all over the world taking pictures of the action and it must have been around this time when the famous picture of me was taken. I was in Pest at the time and the photo shows me standing with my gun in Barrros Place. My brother Peter gave this photo to Anna Ambrosy while she was writing her book. Peter had seen this photo and other ones of me published in Australian newspapers in 1958 and recognised me.

Anna had visited Hungarian clubs that were set up after the uprising by the immigrants: she heard their stories and wanted to write about the uprising. She thanks Peter on page vi of *A Brave Nation* under Acknowledgments she states 'I would also like to extend my appreciation to Peter Nadasdy, a former Corvin Lane Freedom Fighter, for contributing a photograph of his younger brother who, at the age of fourteen, was also a Freedom Fighter.' The photograph appears on page 112 with the caption *Fourteen-year-old Freedom Fighter*. Peter contributed many of his experiences

of the uprising to Anna whilst she was writing her book.

Anna later signed a copy of the book for Peter. He gave the same photos to writer Eva Orban. Peter had no idea that I was involved in the uprising as an active freedom fighter until he saw the photos of me. It was this that prompted him to post the signed books to me from both authors and ask me about my involvement. He had no idea that I had also been involved, because on 23rd October 1956 when he heard the crowds shouting, he left home early to see what was going on. I didn't know where he was and I left the flat later, with my own friends.

Sadly, neither of us knew where the other one was, not even where he went to when he fled from Hungary. Mum knew that he had had to leave and told me this, but she didn't know what we had been doing during the uprising, only that we had been away from home for two weeks. It was safer for mum not to know too much. It wasn't until the 1990's that Peter and I were able to share our experiences about 1956, long after he saw photos of me as a freedom fighter: it was good for Peter and I to be able to talk about it.

Anna Ambrosy had emigrated to Australia from Hungary in 1949. She decided to write her book about the uprising because since 1994 she had been in touch with Freedom Fighters who had emigrated to Australia. She wrote: "It was a 7 year labour of love!" Peter posted a copy her book to me when it was published in Melbourne in 2001. The author wrote inside my copy: "Gyorgy Nadasdy to the former young vibrant Freedom fighter of the 1956 Hungarian Uprising with my entirely acknowledgement."

The following text is from a book written by Eva Orban[1] who had signed a copy for Peter, which reads: "Nadasdy Peter. Many regards to old, special friendships, from Eva Orban" Peter was able to give the author much information about our activities in the uprising.

My photograph is also in this book published in 2006, on page 73 (this photo is reproduced on page vi of this book).

The photographer described what I was doing in Hungarian on that page and it translates like this:

"**As ekszerbolt osszetort a baross teren**. (Jewellery shop at Baross Place.)"

At Baross Place where this picture was taken there was an expresso café called **Zona** and next to it a large, famous jewellery shop. It was all smashed up and windows were broken. Outside stood a small young boy with a rifle, standing with legs apart. On his feet were broken shoes. Around him there was gold and silver jewellery on the floor. He did not touch any of it and also stopped other people getting any of it. He looked after it until the shopkeeper came and collected all the jewellery. He thanked the boy. They became the home side's defence (Home Guard.)"

There wasn't any looting during the uprising – the people were all pulling together and guarded where we could. We were given food by men and women wherever we were, because they know that we were Freedom Fighters and we did not steal food or goods. We were given whatever food there was to spare, by others. We never took advantage of unmanned shops. Our goal was to get the Russians out and to have a new, fair government in. I was proud to have been able to guard the shop that day for a few moments until the shopkeeper came back, yet no one challenged me to try to take anything (probably because I had my gun!). I was just making sure and guarding the shop.

Eva Orban went onto write a set of three volumes of books called called IGAZSAGOT '56-NAK! (True '56 history) in 2011 in which she uses the same photo again in Volume II on page 154, where I am looking sad and staring down the street.

My brother Peter gave photographs of me to Eva Orban for her book. On page 145-6 she asks Peter some questions about my childhood. Peter and I had been in touch many times by 2011 when the three volumes of books had been published and so he was able to answer the author's questions.

In Volume 2 (on page 145) and Volume 3 (page 487) is the heading *A pesti srac akinek fenykepe bejarta a vilagot* which means "A city boy from Pest whose famous photo travelled around the world." The next paragraph, which Peter told Eva Orban about, translates as:

Gyorgy Nadasdy is one of those city lads and his well-known image, which was taken by a BBC photographer in 1956 during the revolution, travelled around the world. He was wearing a large black coat, a black hat and on his back was a rifle. He had an innocent teenage face: a Pest boy who had become a legend. He did not realize that he was being photographed. The city boy lived in Area VII of Pest in Dembinszky utca (Street).

In Peter's words:

"We (Peter and Gyorgy) lived opposite to where there was an Animal School and Hospital, which was like a Veterinary. In the houses near to us there were lots of boys and men who were fighting with guns and weapons to help the country. 50 years later,

[1] Eva Orban *Amit '56-rol mindenkinik tudia kell* (The Truth About '56,) published by Pro Patria in 2006.

Kossuth tér, the Hungarian Parliament building on bank of the Danube, where the shooting began in 1956.
(*Photo*: Szász Pál, Wikipedia)

on the anniversary of the uprising, that was the first time that I met my brother **in our own country** and we went to the celebration to share memories with each other. He lives in England now. When we met others from the Freedom Fighters, they called me (Peter) "little Pedro." We were all pleased to see each other. October 23rd 2006 was the anniversary of what happened and everyone met to talk about it and exchange what we all remembered."

Peter was also one of those city lads "pesti srac". His recollections were gathered from personal conversations beginning in 2004.

These are the questions that Eva Orban asked Peter and his responses as recorded in her book.

Would you say a few words about Gyorgy's childhood?

Gyorgy was born on 17th September 1942. He grew up in Pest and was 7 years in detention. When he came out he went back home and went to work in a bus factory, IKARUS.

We really lived in very poor times. We lived with my mother and younger brother in the flat in Dembinszky utca. He didn't know much about his dear father; he hardly knew anything because dad worked long hours from morning until night. He died very early when Gyorgy was still a very young boy. There were problems with dad and the government. He didn't like communism and got arrested, put into jail where they beat him up and he was only home for a week before he died of thrombosis.

Why did Gyorgy end up in detention?

Gyorgy stole a siphon bottle to get the money to give to mum to help her and the communists put him in detention for 7 years.

Where did Gyorgy spend the 7 years for the theft?

He was at a detention place called Degen, from there moved to Abonyban, where he made friends with a Greek boy. He was a very good friend of his called Delkosz Jorgosz. While they were in detention they were good pals and used to go here and there together. This boy asked Gyorgy lots of times to take him home to our mum because he spoke lots about her: he liked the sound of mum very much. (Gyorgy used to see his mum for a week each year and took Delkosz home with him.) When trouble started he went and found out where he lived and took him to meet the freedom fighters. Both of us wanted to fight the communists.

Where was Gyorgy in October and what happened?

This time he was at home because the 7 years in detention for theft had finished. He was 13 when he was let out and in September became 14 in 1956. He went as apprentice in bus factory called IKARUS in September. October 23rd is when the uprising started.

Now Gyorgy carries on with his own story...

At the moment that the photo was taken, I was staring across the street, looking so very sad and devastated about the present situation. There were many other freedom fighters as young as me, or even younger, who were all just as sad and bewildered about the situation that we found ourselves in. At the Animal School near to where we lived there were lots of boys who fought with rifles and machine guns to defend our fellow Hungarians.

Delkosz and I went to a building where there were some army uniforms that I changed into, including an army hat.[1] I got dressed and went out into the street to show off my new outfit: that was a huge mistake!

The clothes resembled a Russian solder so the Hungarians kept shouting "Russki!" and "Dirty Russian!" and started shooting at me! I immediately ran back into the house and changed back into my old outfit. I was very lucky; thank God that everything was alright. I think that He was looking down on me.

Other Freedom Fighters made us petrol bombs (Molotov cocktails) to throw on the tanks and armoured cars. When they exploded it went into the tanks and jeeps, and Delkosz and I saw the soldiers getting out, burning and screaming. When they were out of the vehicles, we and other people started shooting at them: some died, some were badly hurt. We had to do it because they were killing innocent people, young and old, and the Russians had left them lying dead in the streets all over the city. It was so sad, tragic to see it all, really horrifying. What they did made us very angry and bitter, so it was a case of them or us.

At one place I obtained a machine gun and soon learned how to use it: I shot a Russian soldier with this gun. What happened was that I saw a man's body lying in the street, half on the pavement and half on the road.

Over him stood a little boy crying "Wake up Daddy, wake up!" In the distance there was this Russian soldier grinning. He had shot the boy's father so I shot him! The man may have only been injured but there was no movement. There wasn't much reaction after this as the Freedom Fighters around Delkosz and I were just concerned about the little boy. There was a crowd around the little boy; someone found out where he lived and they took him back into his family home. It was all over very quickly. I could not bear it because I had a little brother, Pisti, who looked about the same age as him, three years old.

---

[1] The photo of Gyorgy in a Russian outfit at Barros ter is from a booklet written/edited by Horvath Miklos, Marton Matyas & Mosonyi Laszlo, *1956 Esemenyei terkepen es kepeken* (What happened in 1956 map and pictures) published by Honvedelmi Miniszterium Terkepeszeti Kozhaszmu Tarsasag, Budapest 2006, p.18 captioned *Egy 'Pesti srac'* (one town boy).

Later on during those two weeks of fighting, my friend Delkosz and I moved onto a place called Corvin ter, which was a small, shady square where there were statues, a cinema, public houses, cafés and meeting places. There were lots of troubles in this area, with Russian tanks and people shooting at the Russians. Just by chance I grabbed Delkosz and pulled him to the floor as there was an enemy soldier pointing a gun at him. As luck had it, a lady Freedom Fighter shot the Russian and we went over to her and thanked her for saving Delkosz's life.

We then moved to the large building at the back of Corvin ter where there were other Freedom Fighters. A man shouted at me saying, "Give me that gun!" I said, "No, it's mine!" He was very angry with me and said firmly that he was in charge here. I still told him "No" and a man near to me told the one in charge to leave me alone. The situation was very tense and he added, "If you don't leave the lad alone I will kill you; that gun belongs to the boy that is holding it." What none of us knew was that there were many secret police around: those people were communists called "AVH"– they killed many Hungarians, their own people.

They were as bad as the Russians, but the Freedom Fighters soon recognised them, hanged and torched them in the streets, openly. The man in charge was one of those State security police, an AVH. Some AVH changed sides but they couldn't win, because if they changed their loyalties from the Russians to the Freedom Fighters, the Communists hanged them. I saw some horrible sights that gave me nightmares. The AVO later became the AVH.

Sadly, Delkosz and I parted as he wanted to try to get back to Greece, but I don't know whether he ever made it there. I eventually went home after about two weeks: it was now November time, and the times were still very troubled. Mum asked no questions of me.

By this time people were hiding because there were several communists living in our block and they would report to the AVH who took part in the demonstrations and uprising. They would have come to arrest us.

There were many ugly scenes in Budapest.[1]

Despite a so-called ceasefire, no-one felt safe. I knew that people were fleeing the country because they were shouting about it, especially the ones who took part in the uprising, and so that is why I knew I had to go from Hungary because it would have been dangerous to stop at home. The communists were going to different places in Budapest to arrest those who had been involved in the fighting.

The reason is because many communists lived in the same blocks as we did and we were able to know who were communists, because they didn't join us to go to fight. As we weren't at home for many days they knew who the fighters were and would have called the State Police or the AVH. If I had stayed I thought I would have been arrested, shot or put in jail; the communists had no mercy! They lived far better lives than the ordinary people did, and had control over us.

When the communists and Russians took over once more, on 4th November 1956, I knew that I must flee; I had gone home with my gun for just a couple of nights and Peter had already left quickly around the middle of November. I went soon after that. Before I left I needed to get rid of my gun; under the apartments there were cellars and I

---

[1] There were many lynchings and beatings by the crowds and in almost all cases the victims were members of the AVH or those believed to have co-operated with them. *Source* UN Report (see Appendix 3 on page 96).

buried my gun in the cellar and after that I left for the border. I left in what I was wearing: a warm coat, but no food or drink. I followed the rest of the people who were leaving the country. It took a couple of days to get to the border, as we had to keep hiding from the communists. There were many different groups of us in bits and pieces, and we kept together. There wasn't much to eat; we slept in bushes or down the side of road (not much traffic in those days, hardly any at all), which was near to the tracks: we knew that this led to the border.

We slept around the railway station, hiding where we felt safe. We travelled by train as well as walking during the night. It took about two days to get to the border. There were people who had bits of food who shared it with me as I was by myself. We were hungry all the time. We kept going because we had to. We would have been arrested and put away. Who knows what could have happened to us.

By the time we reached the border, it was closed and the guards were arresting refugees. I was lucky to get in with a family who knew that I was by myself; the man in this group was also lucky because at the border his brother was the border

The 1956 Eternal Flame monument in Budapest. (*photo* Petr Šmerkl, Wikipedia)

guard. He turned a blind eye and let us go through. What a favour, we were so grateful, but he wasn't going to arrest his own brother and family!

Many Freedom Fighters and families who had not been involved with the revolution were leaving Hungary at this time, as we were all aware that it was unsafe to stay. The men and families that had not been fighting left Hungary because they just wanted a better life away from communism.

Although I was only fourteen at the time I knew that the AVH were not to be trusted and I had to get away. Rumours of people going missing were rife; these were frightening times. It wasn't until I read the books sent to me by my brother in 2006 on the 50th Anniversary of the Uprising that I realised how right we both were to leave Hungary. Many people went missing, were deported to Russia or executed: men, women and even children younger than fourteen. There was a real purge from November 1956 until two years later, to rid Hungary of all those involved in the Revolution and to find the people who acted as witnesses to the Council, who gave information, as accurately as possible, to the United Nations Report. No one was safe.[1]

---

[1] See Appendix 5 for details about deportations.

Hungarian actor Imre Sinkovits reads out the proclamation of university students at the Petofi statue in Budapest on 23rd October 1956, the day that revolution broke out. (*Source* MTI/Tamas Fenyes.)

23A Peaceful demonstration around 25th –26th October. Anna Ambrosy "A Brave Nation" page 104.
(Photo source unknown)

The fateful protest at Bem Square on 23rd October 1956. *Source* Americanhungarianfederation.org/1956

The crowd went to the Parliament Building to initiate talks with government but gunfire from inside the building and Russian tanks killed an estimated 150-200 and wounded many more on 25th October 1956 in Kossuth Square (known as the 'Bloody Thursday' massacre.) *Source* AllWorldWars.com by Major Zoltan Virag and MFA.gov.hu (*photo* Alamy)

The Stalin statue about to be toppled by protesters.
Source: Iconicphotos.files.wordpress.com. 1956 John Sadovy

At the Rakoczi Street/Grand Boulevard intersection (Budapest 8) the Stalin statue is cut up. (*Photo:* Fortepan.hu)

The monument is defaced and dismantled on 23rd October 1956.
Source: Americanhungarianfederation.org

All that remained of the Stalin monument on 24th October 1956.

Source: Americanhungarianfederation.org

ÉKSZERBOLT a Baross téren

A Baross téren egy döbbenetes kép fogadott. Volt egy Zóna nevű presszó, és mellette egy hatalmas ékszer bolt.

Az ékszerbolt összetört üvegű kirakatában egy kis fiatal gyerek állt géppisztollyal, szétvetett lábakkal. A talpánál, a kis csóró szakadt cipője mellett ott hevert a csomó arany. És nem nyúlt hozzá. Az a hozzáállás, hogy vigyáz a forradalom tisztaságára, hogy nem szabad lopni. Ez valami csodálatos felemelő érzés.

(Sz.B.)

"Jewell on Baross Square." A reporter photographs Gyorgy.

Source: page 73 of Eva Orban's book *Amit '56-rol mindenkinek tudia kell*. (Photo source unknown)

Painting featured in the Hungarian Army Museum exhibition about the revolution, copied from the *Life* magazine photo by an unknown artist.

Gyorgy in Russian outfit at Barros ter (Place) with machine gun.

Source: *1956 Esemenyei 56 terkepen es kepeken* (What happened in 1956 with map and pictures) p.18

Original caption: Egy 'Pesti srac'. (One town boy)

Gyorgy with a member of the AVH (who tried unsuccessfully to get Gyorgy's gun off him) at Corvin Ter (Corvin Lane) on October 29th when the revolutionaries were discussing a ceasefire with the government.

Source Newspaper of the time. (Photo: Erich Lessing.)

Corvin Ter (Lane), the area of trouble near to the Picture House, during the siege time.
Source Americanhungarianfederation.org/1956

34 Corvin Lane during a short respite from the siege.
Source: A Brave Nation page 131. (Photo source unknown).

Destruction to Kilian Barracks in November, after the 2nd Soviet attack. (Photo source unknown)

A shattered Soviet tank on Jozsef Circle near Corvin Lane, taken on 27th October 1956.
Source: page 145 of Anna Ambrosy's "A Brave Nation." (Photo source unknown)

Csepelians go to Kilian Barracks. *Source:* americanhungarianfederation.org

Demonstrators with the Hungarian National Flag, around 28th October 1956. (Photo: Lajos Meszaros.)

On a building in Kalvin Square the graffiti reads: 'Russians go home'.
(*Photo* Fortepan.hu)

RUSZKIK HAZA.
РУССКИЕ ДОМОЙ!

Scenes of destruction from the siege of Budapest.

Source 'A Brave Nation'.

Ruined buildings at Jozsef Boulevard, Budapest in November 1956 after the 2nd Soviet attack.
(Photo: Fortepan.hu/Nagy Gyula)

Soviet howitzer on Ferenc Boulevard, November 1956. (Photo: Fortepan.hu/Nagy Gyula)

Local residents watch a column of Soviet military vehicles led by a tank roll along Stalin Street (now Andrassy Street) as the Russians withdraw from Budapest on October 28th 1956. Five days of peace followed. (MTI Photo/Tamas Fenyes)

Soviet tanks re-enter Budapest on November 3rd/4th 1956 to crush the popular revolt.

Source: *All World Wars* by Major Zoltan Virag & Americanhungarianfederation.org

Soviet tank destroyed on Moricz Zsigmond Square. (*Photo*: Fortepan.hu)

Soviet tank destroyed at Corvin Place behind Kilian Barracks, where the fighting was concentrated.
(Photo: Fortepan.hu/Nagy Gyula)

The shattered Kilian Barracks on the corner of Ferenc Avenue. Two weeks beforehand Peter Nadasdy and other Freedom Fighters had been given machine guns, rifles and ammunition from here on 23rd October 1956. *Source* "1956 Esemenyei 56 terkepen es kepeken". (Photo source unknown)

The Hungarian radio building on Brody Sandor Street was also the scene of heavy fighting. (Photo: Fortepan/Nagy Gyula)

From top to bottom

Gerely Pongratz, a Corvin Passage Freedom Fighter leader. *Source* Salamon Konrad, *Tizenket Nap Szabadsag 1956*, p. 127.

Mr Imre Nagy made a final appeal to the West for help at 5.15 am on 4th November 1956. (*Photo* American Hungarian Federation)

Major General Pal Maleter, Minister of Defence; executed by Soviets in 1958 because he was on the side of the insurgents. (*Photo* Americanhungarianfederation.org)

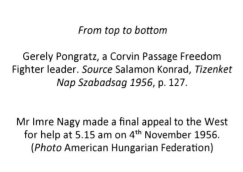

The bodies of two Russian soldiers beside their wrecked armoured car in a Budapest street. (Photo: Alamy.com)

Unarmed civilians shot by Hungarian border guards on Oct 26th 1956 at Mosonmagyarovar (158km NW of Budapest.) *Source* MFA.gov.hu (*Photo* MTI)

Street graves in Budapest. (*Source* Szegedmar.hu / Fortepan.hu)

Hungarian refugees make their way across the border to Austria.

Photos American Hungarian Federation
Americanhungarianfederation.org

Austria

THE RUSSIANS KNEW that I had taken part in the uprising so I had to get away. After walking day and night with others, to get out of Budapest, I managed to board a train in Hungary. This was soon after the 18 days of uprising, which had ended around 10th November.

By this time, huge numbers of Soviet tanks had poured into the country and armoured units were in control on the Danube bridges. We wanted to get out of the country get to Austria, via a Hungarian border town and it had to be during night time. On the train were many Freedom Fighters making their way towards the outskirts of Hungary to flee the country. I went with them to Austria and stayed there until just after Christmas, in early 1957.

This first journey involved us getting the train from Hungary to the Hungarian border. The Freedom Fighters had to leave the train well before crossing the Hungarian and Austrian border to avoid being caught by the Russians and the State Security Border Police, so we left the train and crossed a frozen lake and a fairly shallow river in order to get into Austria. This walk took several hours and we finally ate something when we arrived in Austria. We were all very cold and hungry. We were met on the other side by uniformed Austrian border guards who collected us together and took us to the refugee camp.

We stayed in Austria and were met by people who were expecting us to arrive, as they knew about the uprising. This was a grim time because we had nothing, split from our families and unsure of the future. We were free, however and relieved to be safe, grateful to be rescued by the Austrians.

We were taken into an Army Camp where many Hungarians stayed for a few weeks and were put into different programmes. Older ones sometimes went out of the camp to do paid work, whereas the younger ones like me were entertained by singing or learning, or just amusing ourselves somehow. We younger ones were taught English because we were waiting for sponsorship from an English speaking country that would take us in. The English teacher was a young Austrian lady called Kay Kerzmane. We all loved her because she was so good. She felt sorry for me and took me home to her family and I had a lovely Christmas.

The family had a TV, which was a novelty. I had never seen a TV properly until I was in Austria. We just had a small radio in Mum's house, as only the rich and some of the Communists could afford a TV. I also saw toothpaste and toothbrushes for the first time here, in Austria. We didn't have any in Hungary in our house, but my teeth didn't suffer so they must have been strong! We used to chew on parsnips, carrots, apples and pears, which kept them clean.

This teacher and her family took me to Vienna and bought me new long trousers and a new pair of socks and shoes that I had never had new in my younger days because we were too poor: I will never forget it.

The Austrian people were very kind to us, giving us food, shelter and freedom.

In January, after Christmas I decided to go back to Hungary to try to get my sister, her husband and their son to flee the country with me but they stayed behind. I travelled straight to my sister's house but when they said they couldn't leave, I had to leave straight away because it would have been dangerous to stay. They both had their own jobs and young son. I didn't see Mum as I had already said goodbye the first time I left, and there were communists in the tenement block. They had said "When it finishes (the Uprising), we will get you and your brother Peter. You will both be shot or put in jail for a long time." My brother had said goodbye to my mother and quickly left the house, because he was afraid of the threats made.

I didn't dare go back home. In 1957 more people were trying to get out whom I teamed up with. The borders were now closed by January 1957. The Russians had closed the borders around 14th November 1956.

I started the journey back to Austria. I was lucky to get out of Hungary this second time, with a handful of people, as the Border Guards still turned a blind eye. Again we travelled by train and did much walking as before, though this time we travelled a different route through woods. We had to leave the train very much before the border of Hungary. We left the train and stayed hidden amongst other passengers and started walking like before. We had to get food wherever we could and stopped a couple of times; sometimes farm workers gave us some food. We escaped from Hungary and the Austrian Border Guards collected us all from the Austrian side of the border: we were very pleased to have arrived safely. The authorities took us to where other Hungarians were, in an army camp not far from Vienna (see Appendix 6 on p. 107).

I was on my own but some refugees had kept their families together, or were with other friends. What did hurt me the most was that my mother, sister and two brothers were left behind and I had no idea where Peter was. When people in the world realised that the Hungarian refugees needed help, more jobs came in and the people were grateful that they could go somewhere safe in the world away from communism.

As the weeks passed by, jobs used to come in from all over the world and were put onto a board in the Army Camp's hall. We all kept looking at where we could go. I didn't want to go too far away as lots had gone to Australia, America, Canada and quite a few to Europe. I knew that many put their names down to go to Britain, America or Australia. I didn't want to go too far away as I hoped that one day, if I went to Britain, it was nearest to Hungary and one day I could see my mother again.

I put my name down to come to England to be a miner.

A refugee camp in Austria similar to those in which Gyorgy and Peter would have stayed. (*Source* UNHCR)

In most camps there was no running water, which had to be fetched by bucket.

Refugees line up for hot meals supplied by the Red Cross. The British Red Cross arranged for the transportation, accommodation and welfare of 7,500 Hungarian refugees coming to the UK. (*Source* ICRC)

Refugee children of a similar age to Gyorgy in one of the camps. (*Source* UNHCR)

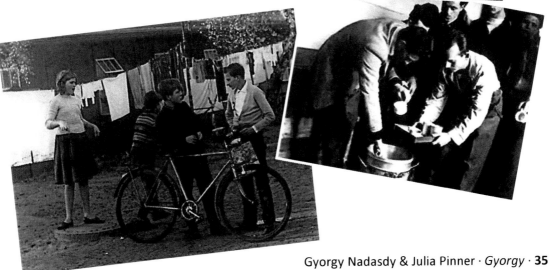

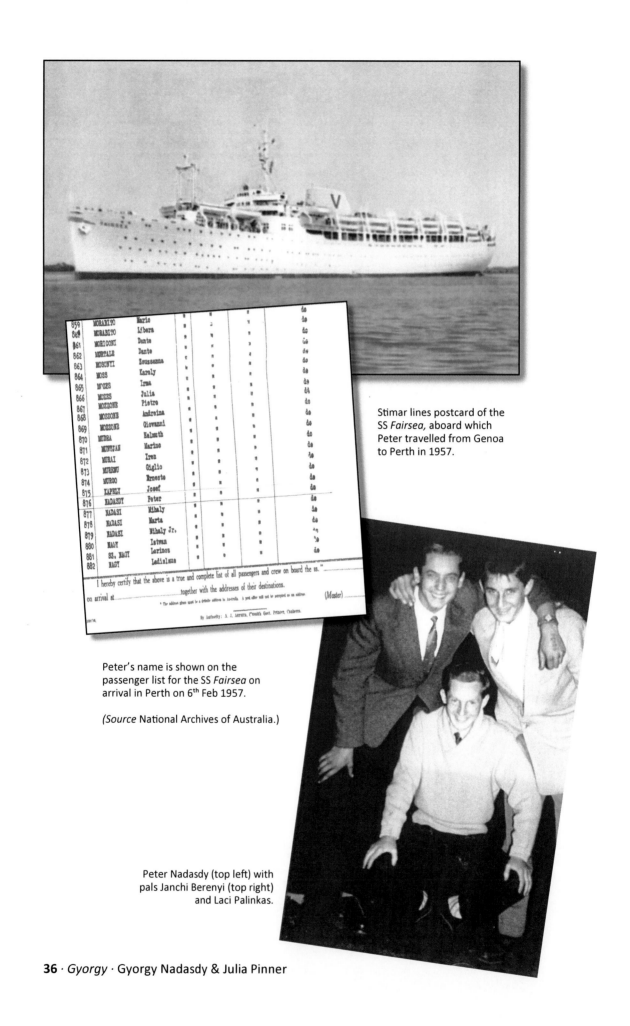

859	MORABITO	Mario				do
860	MORABITO	Libera				do
861	MORICONI	Dante				do
862	MORTALE	Dante				do
863	MOSCNYI	Zsuzsanna				do
864	MOSS	Karoly				do
865	MYZES	Irma				do
866	MYZES	Julia				do
867	MOZZONE	Pietro				do
868	MOZZONE	Andreina				do
869	MOZZONE	Giovanni				do
870	MUDRA	Helmuth				do
871	MUNKYAN	Marine				do
872	MURAI	Iren				do
873	MURENU	Giglio				do
874	MURGO	Ernesto				do
875	KAPELY	Josef				do
876	NADASDY	Peter				do
877	NADASI	Mihaly				do
878	NADASI	Marta				do
879	NADASI	Mihaly Jr.				do
880	NAGY	Istvan				do
881	82, NAGY	Lorincz				do
882	NAGY	Ladislaus				do

I hereby certify that the above is a true and complete list of all passengers and crew on board the ss...................

on arrival at..............................together with the addresses of their destinations.

* The address given must be a definite address in Australia. A post office will not be accepted as an address.

(Master)...................

By Authority: A. J. Arthur, C'wealth Govt. Printer, Canberra.

Stimar lines postcard of the SS *Fairsea,* aboard which Peter travelled from Genoa to Perth in 1957.

Peter's name is shown on the passenger list for the SS *Fairsea* on arrival in Perth on 6th Feb 1957.

(Source National Archives of Australia.)

Peter Nadasdy (top left) with pals Janchi Berenyi (top right) and Laci Palinkas.

Peter's Story

I DISCOVERED LATER THAT my brother Peter and his friend had gone to Australia. Unfortunately, although we were all in Austria at the same time, our paths never crossed because we were in different camps, miles apart. If only I had known where Peter was, I could have contacted him and we might have been together during those nightmare times. Had this been so, our lives in the years that followed would have been very different. As it was, we were to lose contact with each other for 30 years.

As will be revealed in the following chapter, we were reunited thanks to my wife Sylvia, who contacted the production team of the popular TV programme *Surprise Surprise!* in the hope that they might be able to find my brother. They located him in Australia and as a result we met for the first time in 30 years live on British TV!

We have been in contact regularly since then by letter and telephone. I phone him at around 9 o'clock in the morning, when it is the evening for Peter in Australia.

I asked him to tell me everything he remembered about **Tuesday 23rd October 1956** and the events after that, so he wrote it down in Hungarian and posted it to me.

What follows is Peter's story:

Laci lived in the same tenement block as me and Janchi lived in the house next door. Laci, Janchi and I did not go to work that morning because we had heard rumours of an uprising.

Early that evening we went out into the street where we lived and saw a crowd gathering. There were many people, young and old, shouting "pull down that dirty old communist statue of Stalin!" or "Russians go home!" and so forth.

Thousands were already in the streets, students and workers, motivated by the desire for freedom and more were arriving from all directions to march on the town park, where the statue was, about a mile from where we lived. We heard cries from other streets, "Pull him down, the dirty communist!" In the **Varosliget** (or **The People's Square**, now called **Heroes Square**) there were thousands of people gathered around the sculpture, clamouring for its removal.

At about 8pm, three Csepel Hungarian heavy goods lorries arrived, driven by workmen from the southern side of the city. They tied steel ropes around the statue's neck and then the lorries pulled... but, one by one, the three ropes snapped.

The crowd continued to shout "Pull down the dirty old man!" and the lorries pulled again, but the statue did not move at all. Not far away at **Doisa Gyorgy** was an Auto Garage. From there they brought oxy/acetylene cylinders and metal cutting equipment and started cutting through the statue's legs. I had a go with the torching equipment myself, because from time to time the blowtorch was passed around, so that as many people as possible could tell others that they had done some of the work. About thirty of us were involved, all looking forward to see it tumble down!

Eventually we got through the bronze but underneath there were steel reinforcing rods. Sure enough, once these had been burned through, the statue started to give way.

At about 9pm a steel cable was placed around the statue's neck and everyone who could started pulling... A few seconds later, to ecstatic cheers, the effigy of Stalin tumbled to the ground.

Only the boots remained, into which we placed the Hungarian flag.

At about 9.30 two lorries towed the fallen statue via the **Erzsebet** ring road to the corner of **Rackoci Road**, where there was a musical playhouse. Here men, women and children started breaking it up with hammers, saws and pickaxes. Someone in the crowd wanted Stalin's nose as a souvenir; others just broke off any piece they could as a keepsake. People scrawled insulting words over other parts of the statue. This sort of thing you don't read in books!

Later on the news passed through the crowd that there was trouble at the Radio Station in Pest, near to the River Danube, where the Communist Secret Police (AVH) were firing at a crowd of peaceful protesters, mostly students. Trouble had started because the protestors wanted their 16 demands (which had been distributed some hours previously via printed handouts) to be broadcast. The AVH had no intention of allowing this and had opened fire on the protesters, resulting in many casualties.

On hearing this news, many of us made our way to the nearby Kilian Army Barracks in order to obtain guns with which we could fight back at the despised AVH and to defend themselves. My pals Laci and Janchi and I were among those who went to the Barracks. The place appeared to be deserted when we arrived outside its high steel gates. These were locked, of course, but we succeeded in breaking in. I was the first in the queue to get in. There was a nasty scene at the entrance. We were met by some of the garrison soldiers, with rifles and machine guns pointed at us. The officer in charge raised his arm and shouted, "Stop, or we will shoot you all!"

Fortunately, before this could happen, a voice in the crowd shouted that the AVH were killing peaceful protesters and begged the soldiers, "Please help us!"
"In God's name!" someone else said.
The soldiers stood all around us.
"Please help us," we repeated. It was a tense situation but eventually the man in charge said, "Let them go" (and something else that I couldn't hear).

We all breathed sighs of relief and someone said "Sweet God has not forgotten us!"

I later discovered that the name of the Artillery officer to whom we owed our lives was Lajosnak.

The soldiers, who were Hungarian, not Russian, handed over a sizeable quantity of ammunition, old Russian rifles and grenades to us. After thanking them profusely for not firing at us, we loaded a lorry and made our way to Parliament Square, where we distributed the weapons among the protesters. Injured people and dead bodies lay everywhere. Later, the Hungarian Army supported the Freedom Fighters.

We went back to the Radio Station to try to defend the crowd. From 11pm to midnight I was on the first floor of a house opposite the radio station, shooting at the AVH from the window.

Some brave individuals were trying to give first aid to the wounded but they too were shot at. No wonder the AVH was hated. Ambulances arrived, which we were relieved to see, but we were soon to realise that instead of doctors and nurses they contained AVH reinforcements with extra weapons. The crowd pounced upon the impostors. By now the protesters had been armed by Freedom Fighters like us or sympathetic members of the Hungarian Army so could protect themselves from this new threat. The siege of the building started in earnest.

Shortly after midnight Soviet Red Army tanks arrived and intervened in the fighting. There were soon many wounded and dead lying about in the street. The shooting continued all night. With so much gunfire going on all around me, I was fortunate not to be injured.

This is what happened outside the Radio Station in Budapest that night in 1956. Dear God, I will never forget it as long as I live!

The second morning, **Wednesday 24th October**, I also remember very well. At about 9:30 AM the shooting stopped and, after hoisting a white flag, about seven or eight AVH personnel surrendered.

A group of Freedom Fighters went to the House Gate, where the first of the AVH men had surrendered and waited for their colleagues to come down and surrender also. But at about 10am one of the AVH remaining in the building threw a grenade into the crowd. Four or five people died and many more were injured. After that there was no peace.

The leaders of the freedom fighters had written out a list of 16 demands and nailed them to the doors of the parliament building, in the hope that they could get somebody in government to listen. At a park near the Parliament building thousands of men, women and children had gathered, shouting "We want freedom from communism!", "We want to free Hungary!" and suchlike and demanding access to the Parliament Building in order to look at the 16 demands.

From high windows above the crowd the Avosok opened fire with machine guns. About 400-450 people died and hundreds were injured. It took several hours to collect the casualties. There were so many cries of sorrow everywhere. The sights and sounds were sickening.

By ten in the evening the collection of bodies and the injured was over. I was devastated. The other lads and I got into a lorry and went to a place in Pest to get more guns and ammunition to take back to Corvin Place,

where there was a cinema the people called Corvinstak.

On **Thursday October 25th** – "Bloody Thursday" – I was at Kossuth Place. I stood at the Rakoczi Statue and behind me were two young lads. I managed to run across the park with them and stand under a shelter. We decided to wait until things went silent. Here we spoke to other boys and one of them knew another from the Army Barracks, so later on we went there and the soldiers loaded a lorry with guns, grenades and ammunition. We thanked the soldiers, who wanted to help the people but could not get more involved, or they would have been in big trouble.

When we got near to our destination a Russian Tank appeared but fortunately he pointed his spotlight away from us and went into another street. We were lucky that it didn't fire on us, as we were close targets.

By now we could hear the sound of heavy artillery and machine gun fire all around. Several buildings in the city were burning. Our nostrils and throats burned from the smoke. Our bellies were empty. We ran on pure adrenaline. The desire for freedom from oppression, higher living standards, an end to Soviet tyranny, a life free from the worry of AVH visits and arbitrary arrests or secret trials kept us going. This was surely our chance to make Hungary independent and neutral. We wanted to be Hungarian and not be forced to imitate all things Russian. All of us boys were determined and pulled together, following the leader in charge of each area we moved to.

We managed to get to our intended location at Corvin Square, where we were stopped by some of the freedom fighters and asked for a secret code word; I answered correctly and they let us in. The codes were to prevent our ranks from being infiltrated by Russian communists. We rested and had some food, our first for two days. The boys and I thanked them for everything.

On **Friday 26th October** in the early morning we arrived at Corvin Place with more rifles, ammunition and machine guns for the fighters. I was with a boy named Beszkartos and I think he was 2 or 3 years older than me. He was very brave, full of fighting spirit. All night long and the next day, 27th October, there was a lot of gunfire.

My friends and I went to a place called Erszebet where there was a factory which made electric lights. We took some things from here to take back to Corvin Place. Towards the evening, in a road called Hata'r Ut, I met up with a man named Szlama Arpa'd, who was in charge of the Freedom Fighters in this area and asked on him to join us at Corvin Place. Arpa'd was an artillery second Lieutenant in the Hungarian Army who had joined the Freedom Fighters. He and his men had brought tank destroyers and shells by truck from the military garrison at Oroshaza.

Based at the Corvin Cinema, armed with a huge tank destroyer, he and his men put many Russian tanks out of action. People were cheering from streets away when one tank was destroyed and Szlama Arpa'd became famous as the "Hero of Corvin".[1]

It was still the morning of 26th October when we learned that Russian soldiers were just outside Pest, waiting for the command to attack. Also many tanks were arriving.

On Saturday 27th October General Paul Maléter sent in soldiers to disarm the boys in Corvin Place but everyone said (all 64 of us) that we would rather die than give in.

A tank stood outside Kilian Barracks by the first gate. Maléter disarmed the Freedom Fighters in the Barracks and locked them in the underground prison.[2] The Colonel called for the rest of the freedom fighters in the city to surrender and give up their weapons. They refused, so he collected some of the young lads from the Barracks, about twenty of them and put these kids out in a street called Ulloi Road. The Russians and their tanks had taken over this street and when the Young Freedom Fighters tried to run across to

Corvin Place they were fired upon. Many were wounded and several lost their lives.

Afterwards, on Sunday 28th October, there was intense shooting around Corvin Place and when the Freedom Fighters had won this area two Russian soldiers were sent across to have a word with Odon and Gergely (Bajusz) Pongratz (the latter two being the leaders of the Corvin Lane workers and Freedom Fighters) to talk to them. The soldiers told the freedom fighters that they hadn't done any good, nothing had been achieved and there was nothing left.[3]

Nothing else happened after that because Maleter had left the area. He was arrested soon after this date. A ceasefire was announced at this time but it wasn't observed and fighting continued in pockets.

That night Mr Nagy the Hungarian Foreign Affairs Minister announced that Soviet forces would be withdrawn from Budapest.

On **Monday 29th October** I went home to rest and spend a bit of time there. During these last five days I had hardly slept or eaten anything.

Mum was at home. I wonder what her thoughts were? My younger brothers weren't there. I don't know where they were. My mother was quiet; she said nothing but I knew she understood what was going on and why. She was a poor peasant worker who knew the harsh communist system only too well, especially remembering that the KGB had taken my dad in for questioning in 1949 when I was about eight or nine.

On the morning of **Tuesday 30th October** I went to Barros Place to be a National Guard, as it had been agreed that Freedom Fighters should have this position. Then came the news that ten boys had been arrested and were being held in a house in Republic Square, where the Communist headquarters were. We went over there to try to get the lads out; the fighting started that afternoon at about 5pm.

---

[1] *A Brave Nation* page 115. When Hungary lost the war of independence, Szlama was given a 15-year jail sentence and his men were also convicted.
[2] UN Report, 1957.

---

[3] His nickname was *Bajusz*, Hungarian for moustache; he had a large moustache.

As I ran from behind a tree that I had been sheltering behind towards the door of the house I felt a sharp pain in the right side of my body; it was as if the pain was in my bones. I realised that I was wounded. A blast of machine gun fire had struck the cobblestones in the road, sending out a shower of razor-sharp fragments, one of which had hit me in the leg. I was bleeding quite badly and fell over. I felt I was in Hell. I could not stand up.

A young man of about 25, wearing a coloured jacket, picked me up and carried me to a nearby doorway to get medical attention. Later on I found out that he was a French Reporter; I never did find out his name.

I received treatment from a woman who may have been a nurse or another Freedom Fighter, and slowly recovered. This injury slowed me down but I carried on fighting as best I could.

When we Freedom Fighters at last gained access to the house where the ten boys were being held, we got a terrible shock. We found them lying on the floor with bullet holes in the back of their heads. No words can say how we felt.

On **Wednesday 31st October & Thursday 1st November** I spent my time at Barros Place, near to the Railway Station.

We heard that Russian tanks were re-appearing in huge numbers outside Budapest. Then we were re-invaded. Word spread that Soviet forces were entering Budapest in many hundreds of tanks and armoured cars. What chance did we stand now? But the fighting spirit never left us; we did not give up.

On **Saturday 3rd November** at Rakoczi Place near a large building I started fighting again for freedom. A Russian armoured truck was parked up in front of house number 172 and we opened fire and destroyed it.

At one point during the fighting I was near an armoured vehicle when a Russian soldier suddenly stuck his head out of it. I fired at it and blood spattered out. I had killed him. This

is the worst memory of the Uprising for me; it still haunts me to this day.

On the night of November 3rd we congregated in the free peoples building in Pest to find out what we could do next. Many of us had gone up onto the roof of the building. We heard tanks coming from the people's cinema towards the main road, which was just around the corner.

I had been given two petrol bombs, or that's what I thought they were. But I was soon to discover that they actually contained nitro glycerine! The first one I threw down from the roof fell directly onto a tank below. There was a huge explosion. The tank's gun barrel was detached and the tram on the opposite side of the street was blown off its rails. The explosion was so violent that it shook the neighbouring buildings. I was frightened about what the second bomb would do after that, so I gave it to another boy!

During the night we went back to Barros Place where, early the next morning, at around 4am, the fighting started again.

The Russians started firing on us from Kerepesi Road. The boys and I were in one of the rooms on the first floor of a house on the corner of the street. We heard the tanks coming; they were just under the window. Then there was a huge blast between the two windows. The shell hit the wardrobe behind us, which disintegrated. I don't know what it was made out of but fortunately no splinters were generated by the blast. We were lucky that we remained unhurt although we all lost our hearing for a few minutes.

On **Sunday 4th November** the Russian soldiers, who had been arriving since 3rd November in huge numbers with many tanks, attacked us again. The second round of fighting broke out, more fierce and frenzied than ever. The Russians blasted every building. We were hopelessly outnumbered and far less well armed than they were. Budapest was devastated; there was horrendous damage everywhere, like a scene from World War 2. The Soviet guns annihilated everything, everywhere and many Hungarians were buried alive as higher floors collapsed onto lower ones. The air was filled with the sound of tank guns firing, near and far. The ground shook.

On **Monday 5th November** I went home to rest. Mum was there but no brothers. She still didn't try to stop me from going out fighting because she knew the politics of the situation. Unless you lived under communism, you could never imagine what it was like. The conditions of life were cruel and oppressive. There was never enough food or clothes no matter how hard you worked. We Hungarians were the underdogs in our own country.

Neighbours with radios told me that Prime Minister Nagy and free radio broadcasts had been asking the West for help. Repeated SOS signals had been sent. This was unnerving. There had been a radio silence from 10.30am on 4th November until 8.15pm that night, when transmissions resumed by the Soviet-controlled regime. The world would now know about the rape of our city.

I want to acknowledge one of our number, a soldier who had lost part of his leg in World War 2. This brave man, armed with a 76mm heavy gun, successfully destroyed 8-10 Russian tanks in Corvin Lane.

On 5th November a tank he was trying to destroy shot away the lower half of his body and he died on 17th November at Ulloi Hospital. To his friends and former Corvin Lane fighters, Janos Szabo, whose Freedom Fighter name was **Falabu Jancsi** (Wooden Leg) remains a legendry hero.

On **Tuesday 6th November** some pals and I arrested some Russian soldiers near the Animal Hospital, opposite to where I lived. We took them to Dobe Road Barracks, where they were locked up. Later on it was revealed that they were "Gruz" tank drivers. I think this refers to the area in Russia where they came from.

On **Wednesday/Thursday 7th/8th November** I was at the Royal Hotel, where the fighting continued. The Hungarian officer in charge there was Kiss Kalman. I met him again in Australia, many years later.

At 6pm on **9th November** the Revolutionary Council decided to end the fighting. Our ammunition was almost gone.

At about 10 in the morning on **Saturday 10th November** a car equipped with loudspeakers drove by to deliver the message "Put down your guns and leave, it's peacetime now!"

We all agreed and put down our guns. although there was one stupid man who wanted to kill the three Russian tank soldiers we had arrested on 6th November but the rest of us stood in front of him and would not let him shoot them. I personally took the three soldiers to **Newark Palota**. It was just around the corner, a kind of Russian Barracks. They thanked me and gave me a free pass that came in very useful in the near future.

On **Saturday 10th November** no more fighting took place. Russian rule was back in force. Hungarians were fined if out on the street, or just shot on the spot. We were told to keep away from the areas where there had been fighting and to stay inside. Hungarians had a curfew imposed – we must stay indoors between certain times of the day or we would be shot!

Budapest was completely wrecked and all hope had gone.

These are my Freedom Fighting memories of 1956, recalling all that I went through.

After the Russians had re-established control, thousands of Hungarians tried to leave the country, especially those of us who had been Freedom Fighters. we knew that the Communists would soon come looking for us and that we had to escape over the border to Austria where we would be safe.

I knew that there were communist sympathisers in my block of apartments who knew that Gyorgy and I had taken part in the uprising and that they would almost certainly denounce us to the authorities. We knew that people were being jailed, interrogated, disappeared, executed by firing squad or hanged and that it was extremely dangerous for us to remain. My mother knew this very well and although Gyorgy and I were desperately sad to leave the family, she knew that our only safe option was to go.

I later discovered that after we left the Communists punished our mother by making her move about to a number of different lodgings right up until the 1970s, including over the River Danube to Pest. She was questioned by the communist authorities about where we both were. It was a good thing that she truly didn't know. When we left we had no idea ourselves where we would end up. My only thought was to get as far away as possible from Europe and communism, which is why I chose Australia.

At the time I did not know that Gyorgy had been involved in the uprising or that he had left Hungary too. We left at different times and ended up in different places and it would be many years before we were reunited.

I was in a hurry to leave and decided to make for the Austrian border, which was about 100 kilometres away.[1]

I didn't travel with anyone I knew; twenty or thirty of us walked over mountains and through the countryside at night, under the cover of darkness, until we reached the border. We were very cold, hungry and tired; there had been nothing to eat but few bits of dry bread which sympathetic Hungarian people had left out for us. They knew that we had been involved in the uprising so they gave us anything that they could spare.

We eventually came to some railway tracks, where a train driver slowed down to let us all aboard and take us to place near to the Austrian border. The drivers were sympathetic to the refugees and slowed the train several times to let hundreds of migrants aboard. There wasn't much talking between us; we were all exhausted, cold and hungry.

The train slowed again to allow us to jump off just before it reached Sonpron, a city near the Austrian border. Russian guards were there so we had to be cautious. We made our way across country to the border town of Nagycenk. It's difficult to remember how long this journey took: I think it was two days.

Our group was spotted by a Russian guard at the border from a distance away and we were shot at. I received a flesh wound to my stomach, but nothing serious. I was lucky.

On **November 21st** I finally crossed the border into Austria at a small village called Nagycenk in Hungary. After crossing the border we had to wade through a small river, about 10 metres wide but not deep; it only came up to my waist but was very cold. The Austrian Border Guards were sympathetic and kind to us, and greeted us warmly. This area used to be Hungarian territory so many people there spoke our language and understood the situation. (Some territories changed hands after the Second World War, and this affected the borders.)

We walked to the nearest town, where we were taken to the local church and schools. Eventually we were taken by trucks to a French Army Camp in Bludenz, where we were treated very well. I didn't stay in the camp for long, about two weeks. At last we felt safe, had regular good food and somewhere to sleep; it was great. The people in the camp didn't necessarily know each other; all we had in common was that we were escaping a communist regime for better lives in a free country. I put my name down to go to Australia.

Travel by train was arranged for a great many refugees from the camp in Austria to Genoa, Italy. The journey took about six hours and no one was in charge of us nor escorted us at all. We were given food at the stations because by now the world knew the situation in Hungary.

On **January 3rd 1957** I boarded an Italian ship called SS **Fairsea**, which sailed from Genoa, Italy to Freemantle, Perth, Australia via the Cape of Good Hope. We could not go

[1] 17 *A Brave Nation* page 165 "A great terror followed the revolution. Hundreds of people were sentenced to death, while others received long and short-term prison sentences, or were transported to perpetual slavery. In addition, about 200,000 refugees left Hungary, with a detrimental effect on the already decimated population of Hungary.

through the Suez Canal due to trouble there at that time.[1]

There were refugees on board the ship from many different countries including the Hungarians heading for a better life. I was able to talk about the experiences of the Uprising now; it was good for us to exchange stories and get it out in the open. It helped us all to talk, no good bottling it up.

I have already described my worst moment, when I shot the Russian soldier on 3rd November 1956. Although he would certainly have fired at me had I not shot first, it still haunts me now.

Now my best moment. It was when I boarded the SS **Fairsea**, knowing that I would be safe, tasting delicious food in first class accommodation and was even given a bottle of wine!

On **13th February,** 41 days later, I set foot for the first time in Australia, where we all received a warm welcome.

The **Fairsea** docked at Freemantle, Perth then later sailed to Melbourne, where fellow Hungarians met us. The locals in Melbourne were very friendly. I liked it there.

We were taken to Melbourne's Army Camp, where many stayed for two months. I was only there for two weeks. Just as we had done when we were on board the ocean liner, we enjoyed good food and safe lodgings. We were even given cigarettes! Many Hungarians had emigrated to Australia after the Second World War and these people now helped us to find work and lodgings, making it easier to settle down. They were an older generation to us and most of them are now dead, but I will always remember their kindness. They were able to speak to us in our own language,

which was a great advantage, since most of us knew very little English.

Within two months of arriving in Australia I wrote a letter to Mum. I later discovered that she had received the letter but when she tried to post a reply to me, it was censored. I didn't receive anything; no letters were ever allowed to get through. I did not see her again until many years later, when I finally returned to Budapest. The complete joy of seeing my mum and sister and brothers was wonderful, indescribable.

Hungarian clubs were formed by some of the thousands of refugees who came to Australia from Hungary after the Uprising and thanks to these clubs, quite soon after arriving in Australia I was reunited with my pals from Budapest, Laci Palinkas and Jancsi Berenyi.

Many years later, at one of these clubs, I met a lady called Eva Orban, who had lived in the same block of apartments as us in Budapest. She was collecting personal accounts of the Uprising from former Freedom Fighters, myself included and wrote a series of books about it.

By this time my brother Gyorgy and I had been reunited and I purchased copies of all of her books to send to him in England; she signed the copies with a personal message.

I have lived in both Sydney and Melbourne. In those early days crowds of us Hungarian refugees went to Queensland to work under a contract for £20–25 a week in the sugar cane fields. Many different nationalities worked here. The pay was excellent but the work was hard, sometimes a 10-hour day using just a machete and our arms – no machines! By trade I am a Panel Beater but this was good money and helped me to settle. Eventually I came back to live in Melbourne, which I prefer to Queensland. I later became an Australian citizen.

So, Gyorgy, this is what I remember.

---

[1] Melbourne Steamship Co Ltd were the agents named on the passenger list. SS *Fairsea* was the first passenger ship of the Sitmar Line. It was built in 1949 and a contract was obtained from the International Refugee Organisation (IRO) before it began life as migrant ship providing basic accommodation for 1,800 passengers with the intention of transporting emigrants from Europe to Australia. In 1955 *Fairsea* was chartered by the Australian government to transport assisted immigrants from Britain (known as 'Ten Pound Poms').

Anna Ambrosy signed a copy of her book for Gyorgy: *"Gyorgy Nadasdy to the former young vibrant Freedom Fighter of the 1956 Hungarian uprising with my entirely acknowledgment. Anna Ambrosy."*

Add tovább utódaidnak!
„Megcselekedtük, amit megkövetelt a Haza"

Eva Orban signed the copy of her book that Peter purchased:
"Nadasdy Peter. Many regards to old, special friendships, from Orban Eva."

Radio Pleas for Help

GYORGY DID NOT know about the events described in the next three chapters because at the time he was in the refugee camp in Austria. But the world knew about the Hungarian Revolution, various radio broadcasts from Budapest ensured that. It was reported by many sources globally, including Pathe News, American programmes and in Australia.

The BBC reported on 23rd October 1956: "Hungarians rise up against Soviet rule." The next BBC news, dated 26th October stated: "Hungarian Revolution Fighting Spreads" and, on 4th November, "Soviet Troops Overrun Hungary."[1]

The *Times* newspaper also made reports.

On 4th November at 5.20am Premier Nagy made the following statement from Free Radio Kossuth, Budapest:

"...Today at day break Soviet troops attacked our city with the obvious intention of overthrowing the legal Hungarian democratic Government. I notify the people of our country and the entire world of this fact...I ask that all the leaders should turn to all the peoples of the world for help..."[2]

On 28th October, the Austrian Interior Minister had already correctly assessed the situation that would ensue as the uprising, and had been proactive in sending the following message to London, Paris and Washington:

"To all appearances, the uprising in Hungary will come to an end following massive Soviet military intervention. In that event, it can be presumed that larger Hungarian armed formations will cross into Austria."

This certainly happened and by 4th November, 5,000 refugees had already crossed the Austrian border. The Austrian Minister, Mr. Oskar Helmer sent another cable for help. By 6th November, the number had doubled to 10,000 refugees.

Austrian Interior Minister, Oskar Helmer. On 4th November, Helmer sent an urgent cable to the headquarters of UNHCR and of the Intergovernmental Committee for European Migration (ICEM) asking for help, both in the form of financial assistance and in assurances that most of the refugees would be quickly moved on out of Austria.[3]

In total, more than 200,000 people left Hungary after the failed Uprising.

Later that day at 7.57am, The Free Radio Kossuth broadcast this announcement, an appeal by the Hungarian Writers' Union:

---

[1] Ref: 2.3.15. news.bbc.co.uk/on this day.
[2] *A Brave Nation*, page 137-138.

[3] Central Eastern Review: The Welcome Refugees. ce-review.org/99/19/nemes19.html

"We appeal for help to writers, scholars, academics, scientific organisations and leaders of intellectual life all over the world! Our time is limited! You all know the facts; there is no need to explain them. Help the Hungarian people!

This appeal was repeated in English, German and Russian. At 8.07am Free Radio Kossuth went off the air. How crushed the Hungarians must have felt, all hope gone for freedom from Soviet rule and outside help.

Neutral Austria opened its arms to the refugees and acted as their initial rescuers. Austria gave hope to the traumatised Hungarians in their welcome and excellent organisation of the situation.

Also, on 4th November, for one tragic day, the entire world was to eavesdrop upon the battle. In the old Szabad Nep building at the corner of Rakoczi Street and Jozsef Boulevard, the MTI (Hungarian Press Agency) reporter was sitting at a teletype machine when the Russians began their Sunday assault on this area. By a most unlikely coincidence, he had an open wire to the Associated Press offices. This brave young man typed out his report on the death of his city. Deservedly, his words were printed all over the world:

"At the moment there is silence. It may be the silence before the storm. We have almost no weapons, only light machine guns... the tanks are nearing, and so are the heavy artillery... What is the United Nations doing? Give us a little encouragement... the government has not done enough to give us arms.

Downstairs, there are men who have only one hand grenade... The tanks are coming in big lines... It is 10.20am now there is heavy firing near to the centre of the city... Send us any

news you have about world action on Hungary's behalf. Don't worry; we will burn your dispatches as soon as we have read them.

Don't worry about us. We area strong even if we are only a small nation. When the fighting is over we will rebuild our unhappy, much oppressed country."

At 10.30am on 4th November the last message had come through, then the correspondent in the Szabad Nep building was heard no more. Appropriately the message read:

"Just now the heaviest fighting is going on at the Kilian Barracks. There is steady artillery fire."

Later in the day the Szabad Nep building was fired upon at point blank range.

From an unknown freedom radio station, an unknown fighter cried to the conscience of the world:

"Civilised people of the world... the Soviet Army is attempting to crush our troubled hearts. Our women, mothers and daughters are sitting in dread...save our souls. SOS SOS. People of the world, listen to our call. Help us – not with advice, not with words but with action, soldiers and arms. Please do not forget that this wild attack of Bolshevism will not stop. You may be the next victim. Save us SOS SOS. People of Europe... listen to the alarm bells ringing from Hungary. Civilised people of the world, in the name of liberty and solidarity, we are asking you to help. Our ship is sinking. The light vanishes. The shadows grow darker from hour to hour. Listen to our cry. Extend to us brotherly hands. People of the world, save us. SOS Help, help, help. God be with you and with us."

After that there was silence.[1]

These last radio SOS calls on the 4th November were significant. From 4th-11th November the sacking of Budapest took place with savage force as the communists continued to purge the city. The Soviet Army's rule of thumb was... if there was a single shot from any house, destroy the whole house. If there are shots from a street, shoot down every building in the street. Bottom stories were fired at from tanks so that the house fell down upon itself. Thousands of Hungarians were buried alive.

Worse barbarism was still to come. Russian tank crews roared through streets and fired upon any groups of civilians that they saw. Three instances of women in queues were shot to death; Ambulance and Red Cross workers were mercilessly shot down; Nurses

attending the wounded were executed by point-blank rifle fire. All the blood and blood plasma at the Hungarian central depot was confiscated by the Russians and taken to the hospital reserved for them.

Children were killed; hospitals fired upon and young men were executed merely under suspicion. The National Archives were burned out; stores were looted and destroyed by Soviets.

The sacking of Budapest was senseless and unnecessary. A city was ravaged, but the world knew, due to the brave young reporter who typed out the horrifying news from the old Szabad Nep building, the MTI (Hungarian Press Agency).

[1] 23 *A Brave Nation*, pages 156-157.

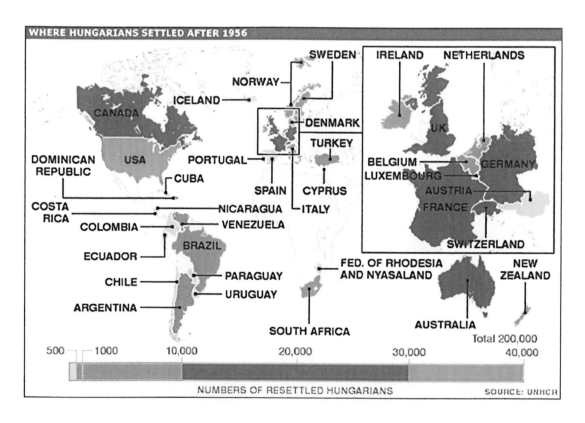

Where Hungarian refugees settled after 1956. (*Source* UNHCR)

International Reactions

THIRTY-SEVEN COUNTRIES RESPONDED with various offers to help after Premier Nagy's plea from the Free Radio in Budapest. Western powers made moving speeches, declarations and promises, accepted large number of refugees, donated aid to Hungary but did not take any steps against the Soviet Union. They were distracted by the danger of military confrontation with the Soviets in another part of the globe and consequently left Hungary to suffer Soviet cruelty alone.

The Suez affair was that distraction. It is possible that Soviet soldiers were initially directed to the Suez Canal area.[1]

The world was well aware of the desperate plight of Hungarians, due to Premier Nagy's statement from Free Radio Kossuth, Budapest on 4th November; the appeal by the Hungarian Writers' Union later that day repeated in English, German and Russian; the MTI (Hungarian Press Agency) reporter who sent a teletype machine message, plus the heart rendering SOS sent from an unknown radio source to the world the same day.

Austria's reaction was amazing, proactive and life saving to thousands of fleeing refugees. The country knew from the outset of the uprising in October, that the next step would be Hungarians crossing Austria's border. At first during this month was only a trickle of refugees. At the news of the desperate savagery inflicted upon Budapest on 4th November, instant action was taken by Austria.

Austrian Interior Minister, Oskar Helmer, on 4 November, sent an urgent cable to the headquarters of UNHCR and of the Intergovernmental Committee for European Migration (ICEM) asking for help, both in the form of financial assistance and in assurances that most of the refugees would be quickly moved on out of Austria.

In November of 1956 Western governments and civilian organizations offered a considerable amount of food, clothing and medical aid to support the Hungarians in Austria. The call of the United Nations general meeting was followed by a worldwide campaign to support Hungarian refugees and help them settle in the West. The United States headed this action and as early as November 2nd offered $20 million in aid to Hungary.[2]

Great Britain responded to the Lord Mayor of London's "Hungarian Appeal" made in November 1956, which spread throughout Britain, supported by local Mayors in all counties.

[1] 24 hungarianhistory.com/lib/anniv56/anniv56.pdf pages 14-19

[2] 25 gabrielkrekk.com/artist-biography-chapter-two.html

There were other reactions to the uprising, from both the Olympics and Elvis Presley!

The Olympics were held in Melbourne in 1956 and this was the first Games boycott. The Soviet invasion of Hungary provoked protests from numerous Western countries and some of them, such as Spain, Switzerland and the Netherlands, withdrew from the games. At the Olympic village, the Hungarian delegation tore down the Communist Hungarian flag and raised the flag of Free Hungary in its place.

A confrontation between Soviet and Hungarian teams occurred in the semi-final of the water polo tournament on 6th December. The match became extremely violent and was halted in the final minute to quell fighting among spectators. Known as the "blood in the water" match, it became the subject of several films. The Hungarian team won 4–0 and later was awarded the Olympic gold medal.

On Sunday 28th October 1956, as some 55 million Americans watched Ed Sullivan's popular television variety show, with the then 21-year-old Elvis Presley headlining for the second time, Sullivan asked viewers to send aid to Hungarian refugees fleeing from the effects of the Soviet invasion. Presley himself made another request for donations during his third and last appearance on Sullivan's show on 6th January 1957. Presley then dedicated a song for the finale, which he thought fit the mood of the time, namely the gospel song 'Peace in the Valley'.

By the end of 1957, these contributions, distributed by the Geneva-based International Red Cross as food rations, clothing, and other essentials, had amounted to some 26 million Swiss Francs (US$6 million, equivalent to $50,400,000

today). On 1st March 2011 Istvan Tarlos, the Mayor of Budapest, made Presley an honorary citizen, posthumously, and a plaza located at the intersection of two of the city's most important avenues was named after Presley as a gesture of gratitude.

Time magazine, in January 1957, made 'The Hungarian Freedom Fighter' its *Man of the Year* and a stylised picture was featured on the front cover of this issue. The magazine states:

"The Man of the Year had many faces, but he was not faceless; he had many names, but he was not nameless. History would know him by the face, intense, relentless, desperate and determined, that he had worn on the evening of Oct. 23 in the streets of Budapest; history would know him by the name he had chosen for himself during his dauntless contest with Soviet tanks."

Australia also took an active role in the situation, shown by the following quotes.

"As a result of these events and particularly the cruel Soviet response, particularly the communist parties, lost a large measure of their support throughout the world, this was felt very clearly in Australia. The people organized demonstrations of support and influenced their representatives in the UN to keep the matter of the crushing of the Hungarian Revolution 'alive' for years.

The Security Council of the UN responded immediately as a result of the Australian initiative. Prime Minister of Australia, R.G. Menzies in a statement on 30th of October expounded the standpoint of his government and questioned the legality of the Soviet action. The Security Council met in emergency session on the 28th October and the 4th and 8th November and in regular session on the 12th November. It kept the Hungarian Question on its agenda until 1962 but the Soviet Union vetoed any decisions it attempted to make widely known in every case, and decisions of the General Assembly were simply disregarded.

Australia (Walker) was an elected member of the Security Council... it was the initiative of the Australian representative, The Australian Government's Security Council and General Assembly in 1956 and subsequent years, made very generous acceptances of Hungarian Refugees.

Hostilities and casualties were horrendous during the second intervention of the Soviets (See Appendix 10). It was reported that guns fired at house after house, destroying them and killing men, women and children even though their fire was not returned. 20,000 flats were damaged, and over 2,000 completely destroyed. There was disregard for the white flag emblem, hands held up in surrender and the Red Cross sign. 2,500 Hungarians and 700 Soviet troops were killed in the uprising and 200,000 Hungarians had to flee the country as refugees.

After the uprising revenge was harsh. Over 350 people were hanged (the official figure is only 229) while an estimated over one thousand were tortured to death and over 22 thousands were jailed or placed into forced labour camps. Over half of those hanged did not take part in the fighting. Their crime was that they accepted membership of workers' councils and thus acted as representatives of the people. The charge resulting in the death penalty being imposed for most of them was 'conspiracy against the socialist state'.[1]

A considerable number of children died in the fighting or were killed in the repression that followed the crushing of the uprising. A large proportion of those who died in the street fighting were teenagers, since the freedom fighters were predominantly below the age of 18 years. There were even some reports of youths being shot in the head immediately after being disarmed. Propaganda had it that those who surrendered would not be harmed but the reverse was true in reality. Once the government felt itself to be strong enough arrests and arraignments started in earnest. Many young people were rounded up from mid-1957 and sentenced to lengthy jail terms or even hanged. Children under the age of 18, according to the law in force at the time, could not be tried in an adult court of law and be sentenced to jail or death by hanging. Capital punishment for minors was against the law for crimes that they might have committed as minors. However the government was not particularly sensitive to such nuances: they simply waited until their victim reached the age of 18 before carrying out the execution. The communist thirst for revenge was limitless. There were 188 young people (students, industrial apprentices, undergraduates)[2]

[1] hungarianhistory.com/lib/anniv56/anniv56.pdf pages 16-17.

The name of the youngest freedom fighter to be executed was Peter Mansfeld. He was just 18 at the time of his death on 21st March 1959, nearly three years after the uprising was over. The brutal government waited until he turned 18 before hanging him the very next day. He was a young worker and the government ordered a lot of party members to watch the event and thereby demonstrate what revenge would be wrought on traitors of the working class. He was hanged but in such a way that he suffocated and that took over 13 minutes. The inhumanity of the communist system was clearly demonstrated by this barbarous act.

He was 15 years old at the time of the uprising and his crime was that he disarmed a policeman. He did not kill anybody. He was a young boy and the 'humane' system showed its true inhumanity. The system demonstrated its power to its own members in order to show its revenge against all traitors to the ideology. Peter was a young worker and the Hungarian Socialist Workers' Party regarded his opposition as treachery.

The refugees represented a cross-section of the population. Many were simple workers, others, highly skilled and educated, were not willing to sell themselves again as slaves to the party bosses. The people were aware of the essence of the 'Promised Land' and freedom in their private life was more important than any level of living standards. However the lure of bettering themselves materially also had mobilizing power. Over 200,000 Hungarians left the country between mid-November and mid-January before the new government in Budapest finally managed to hermetically seal the border again. This was done with a wide

zone of minefields, barbed wire fences and watchtowers along the western border with Austria. Thus Hungary was turned into a huge concentration camp and it remained so for half a decade.

Their first destination of refugees was Austria, which reacted immediately and accepted most of them. Once this route was sealed off many people escaped to Yugoslavia but most were not allowed to proceed further. They were generally returned to Hungary and faced serious charges for illegally crossing the borders. Other countries then resettled the refugees who were in Austria. Most settled in the USA, Canada, Australia and New Zealand and many European countries including Switzerland and Sweden."

In the months following the suppression of the revolution nearly 200,000 people left Hungary. The refugees, before settling down in different Western countries, spent a shorter or longer period of time in Austrian and Yugoslavian refugee camps. Even before 4th November Western governments and civil organizations offered a considerable amount of food and medical aid to support the Hungarians, but only a part ever reached Hungary due to the second Soviet intervention.[1]

In November the call of the UN general meeting was followed by a worldwide campaign to support Hungarian refugees and help them settle in the West. The United States headed this action and as early as 2nd November it offered $20 million in aid to Hungary. It also took generous care of Hungarians settling on its own territory and offered support to other nations taking in refugees. A major part of the

---

[2] hungarianhistory.com/lib/anniv56/anniv56.pdf pages 16-17.

[1] hungaria.org/projects.php?projectid=2&menuid=14, Csaba Békés - János Rainer M. Associates of the 1956 Institute.

maintenance costs of Austrian refugee camps (about 53 were set up) was also covered by the United States.

The majority of Hungarian refugees – about 80,000 people – found new homes in the United States, while 22,000 settled in England, 16,000 in the German Federal Republic, 14,000 in Switzerland and 13,000 in France. New Zealand and Holland accepted just over 1,000 each.

The first refugees arrived in London by plane before 17th November 1956.[1]

Soviet Repressive Measures

A great terror followed the revolution. Hundreds of people were sentenced to death, while others received long and short prison sentences, or were transported to perpetual slavery. In addition, about 200,000 refugees left Hungary. This had a detrimental effect on an already decimated population of Hungary.[2]

The exodus of refugees was in three waves... young adventurers who had heard of the bright lands of the West... the second wave were young people carrying nothing, the average age being twenty five... containing a high percentage of engineers and technicians.

It was the third wave that brought the most refugees and the most problems (of sheer numbers in refugee camps) ...numbering about one hundred and seventy thousand. Many were healthy, middle class people who hated communism and saw a chance to escape. No doubt they wanted to get out ten years ago. This was their chance to escape.

Only about one percent participated actively in the revolution (about 2,000.)

These vast numbers fled Hungary because to remain behind would have been to invite execution or deportation to slave labour camps in Russia.[3]

Gyorgy and Peter were just two people of this one percent who were active in the revolution, to flee the country.

The Refugee Camps of Austria

As the tanks entered Budapest on 4th November the outside world reacted with great speed, despite the competing Suez Crisis. They were not prepared to intervene inside Hungary, but they were prepared to do a great deal for the Hungarians who got out. One of the principal movers and shakers was the Austrian Interior Minister, Oskar Helmer. On 4th November, Helmer sent an urgent cable to the headquarters of UNHCR and of the Intergovernmental Committee for European Migration (ICEM) asking for help, both in the form of financial assistance and in assurances that most of the refugees would be quickly moved on out of Austria.

In Vienna, a committee was immediately set up comprised of Helmer and his staff, UNHCR, ICEM, and the League of Red Cross Societies (LRCS), as well as a number of local and international NGOs. The LRCS would be the prime mover on the assistance front, and would also assist ICEM with registration, documentation and transport of refugees out of Austria. UNHCR would deal with the over-arching legal and protection issues, as well as integration of those who remained in Austria.

---

[1] British Pathe original paperwork reads 17/11/1956.
[2] *A Brave Nation* page 165

---

[3] *A Brave Nation* page 182

In November of 1956 Western governments and civil organizations offered a considerable amount of food, clothing and medical aid to support the Hungarians in Austria. The call of the United Nations general meeting was followed by a worldwide campaign to support Hungarian refugees and help them settle down in the West. The United States headed this action and as early as November 2nd, it offered $20 million in aid to Hungary. It also took generous care of Hungarians settling down on its own territory and offered support to other nations taking in refugees.

A major part of the maintenance costs of Austrian refugee camps was also covered by the United States. This school building would be a holding centre for tens of thousands of Hungarians over the next several months, where each one was registered, examined and then shipped out to refugee camps across Austria. The Austrian government was giving each family 30 shillings a week, which allowed them to make purchases in the local towns and villages for items beyond food, clothing and shelter.

It was as if a dam had broken. A trickle of people had started crossing the border into Austria in the last week of October. The following weekend (4-6 November), 10,000 crossed. By 16th November the total had risen to 36,000 and by the end of November it had soared to 113,000. A further 50,000 in December took the total to 164,000 in just over nine weeks. By the spring, when to all intents and purposes the movement ceased, 180,000 had entered Austria and another 20,000 had sought asylum in Yugoslavia. Food and clothing provided by the Red Cross was plentiful. Each week the clothing trucks would pull in and every person could take what they needed. They lacked for nothing except privacy and a meaningful existence.[1]

Paul Nemes explains how the West opened its arms to fleeing Hungarians in 1956.[2]

As Russian troops, at least officially, were not allowed within five km of the neutral Austrian border according to an international agreement, the Kadar regime was not able to close the border until into the New Year, and Hungarians continued to pour into Austria throughout the autumn and winter. Most refugees came from Budapest and other cities, and far fewer from the countryside.

On 4th November the Soviet armoured attack on Budapest and other major Hungarian cities began. By noon, five thousand Hungarians had already crossed the Austrian border. In total, more than 200,000 people left Hungary after the failed Uprising. Just as they had fought in hope of a US and Western military intervention, Hungarians left for a life in the West they had heard so much about on Radio Free Europe and Voice of America. Although a transit country, it was Austria - a neutral country with no capacity to help Hungary militarily or otherwise - that was the least hesitant to accept Hungarian refugees.

200,000 is a substantial loss for a country of only 10 million, but why did not even more people leave once it became clear that Hungary would remain in the Soviet sphere for the indefinite future? In Communist Hungary, news was hard to come by. Many also thought that a return to the old ways was impossible, and that the Kadar regime would accept this. Even many of the freedom fighters refused to leave, thinking

---

[1] gabrielkrekk.com
[2] Paul Nemes: The Welcome Refugees

that they would escape a long prison sentence or death. Attachment to the land was also strong. Most refugees came from Budapest and other cities, and far fewer from the countryside.

During the weeks of November 4-6th some 10,000 Hungarians entered Austria. Students, teachers, doctors, famous athletes and footballers, farmers, archictects, factory workers and labourers all started streaming into Austria.

It was the first major crisis to appear on television, as well as in the newspapers and on cinema newsreels (British Pathe News) and people across the world were shocked to see the scenes from Budapest and snow covered Austria.

By the time the borders were sealed, 200,000 had fled. (180,000 to Austria and 20,000 to Yugoslavia. Within days of the exodus starting, an extraordinary operation sprang up in Austria, not only to care for the refugees, but to move them out of the country as fast as possible. The performance of the Austrians, the aid agencies and the resettlement countries has rarely, if ever, been matched.

In Vienna, a committee was immediately set up comprising the Austrian Interior minister Oskar Helmer and his staff, the UNHCR (United Nations High Commissioner for Refugees) and the Intergovernmental Committee for European Migration (ICEM) and the league of Red Cross Societies (LRCS) as well as local and international Non-Government organisations (NCO's.)

Within a few days of the first refugees arriving, a massive effort was launched to resettle the Hungarians: over the following months, bus, train, boat and plane

transferred them to 37 different nations on five continents. The United States and Canada each took in around 40,000, while the United Kingdom accepted 20,000 and Germany and Australia some 15,000 each. Two African and 12 Latin American countries also took in Hungarians. The three agencies and NGOs (Non-Government Organisations) put up an exceptional performance.[1]

Differing numbers of casualties are given by sources that I have used. Anna Ambrosy states: "No exact documents or records are available from the unfortunate victims of the uprising. Nobody knows how many persons were executed or died under torture of the AVH prisons; and how many became sick and useless for life. Russia did not record the numbers of their victims, or they never let it be known to the Hungarians. The prison documents had been destroyed by the AVH: these documents definitely would have connected them and discriminate against them by their victims."

In addition, the United Nations Report[2] stated, 'The number of civilian victims was said to be definitely higher than that of military victims.'

According to Kramer, "Two years of intensive 'normalisation' including purges, arrests, deportations and executions, (by hanging) of Nagy and Pal Maleter in 1958, were carried out to eliminate the most active opposition to Kadar's government. By the time the process was completed, more than 100,000 had been arrested, 35,000 tried for 'counterrevolutionary acts', nearly 26,000 had been sentenced to prison, and as many as 600 had been executed".[3]

---

[1] unhcr.org/453c7adb2.html
[2] United Nations Report Munchen 1957: 241
[3] *A Brave Nation* page 188

Lord Mayor Sir Cullum Welch speaks with staff as they process incoming donations. (*Source* British Pathé Ltd)

A donation is placed in the box outside Mansion House in response to Lord Mayor's Appeal. (*Source* British Pathé Ltd)

The Lord Mayor of London's 'Hungarian Appeal'

ON 4TH NOVEMBER 1956 Mr Oskar Helmer, the Austrian Interior Minister, sent an urgent cable to the headquarters of UNHCR (United Nations High Commissioner for Refugees) and to the Intergovernmental Committee for European Migration (ICEM) asking for help, both in the form of financial assistance and in assurances that Hungarian refugees would be moved quickly out of Austria. In Vienna, a committee was immediately set up comprised of Helmer and his staff, UNHCR, ICEM, and the League of Red Cross Societies (LRCS), as well as a number of local and international Non Government Organisations. (NGOs.) The refugees went to 37 different countries.[1]

The result of the Austrian appeal was that many countries agreed to help: the USA and Canada, Germany, the UK, France, Switzerland, Australia, New Zealand, Holland and others.

In the United Kingdom the Lord Mayor of London, Sir Cullum Welch, made a national appeal for help. At Mansion House in London he set up the "National Hungarian and Central Europe Relief Fund." His first target was to raise one million pounds to send to organisations in Austria dealing with the Hungarian refugee situation. In a special Pathé Newsreel released on 19th November 1956 he declared, "They need help. Medical aid, food, transport, clothing and homes." His 'Hungarian Appeal' was sent all over Great Britain, to local organisations and councils.[2]

A further newsreel dated 26th November showed what a great success his appeal had been. The film showed a cheque for £25,000 received from one donor. Lying on top of it is a letter with six sixpenny stamps, totalling 3 shillings, sent by someone else. A letter with coins clipped to it says *'To all the lost children from my own money box'*. It is from 'Rodney' who is 6 years old ,with kisses at the bottom. Another letter with two shillings clipped onto it reads: *'My Lord Mayor I would like to give this 2/- from my pocket money for the Hungarian Relieve Fund'*. The Lord Mayor walks around, watching the good work go on in a room filled with young ladies busy sorting letters and donations.

Other newsreels from that time showed poignant scenes captioned as:

"Street in Budapest with crippled tanks sitting on the roads. Camera pans to show other tanks and two bodies in the foreground. Tracking shot from car, past people watching, showing devastation in the background.

Pan across the front of a building which has been devastated, camera pans down to show a crippled tank outside the building.

---

[1] gabrielkrekk.com

[2] britishpathe.com

Sad people at a funeral. Children standing beside an armed guard at the graveside. Women with head scarves at the grave side, one of them weeping.

The frontier post between Hungary and Austria. Refugees coming towards the frontier including children carrying little bundles.

Refugees on a cart. Women holding children sitting on their belongings. People standing about in a refugee camp in Austria (two shots).

Male refugees drinking from mugs. A Little girl drinking from tin pan. Interior, reception centre showing piles of clothing being issued to a line of refugees.

Refugee woman's face as she selects clothing. A young boy looking bewildered. Little girl's face being held by a woman. TV.

A very small baby wrapped up in a bundle lying on camp bed. Children sitting round table, eating. A group of very young children eating from soup plates. Very little girl eating from a very large plate using a very large spoon."

Tamworth's Response to the Hungarian Aid Appeal

The Lord Mayor of London's Appeal was supported all over Great Britain by local councils, including Tamworth, which was to become Gyorgy's hometown in March 1957.

The Lord Mayor of Tamworth (Councillor E. A. Courts) made his first appeal in the *Tamworth Herald* of 16th November 1956.

Numerous subsequent entries headed *Hungarian Relief Fund* gave updates on the amounts raised. Local people were soon

organising all manner of events to boost funds. According to the *Herald* these included:

"A Whist Drive at Edingale Village Hall on 30th November 1956; collection boxes in clubs and public houses; Tamworth Football Ground; every public house and working men's club in Tamworth; Tamworth Fire Station; the Palace and Grand Theatres in Tamworth; all local schools including Clifton Campville, Tamworth Girls School, Moorgate; Messrs Tolson, Tamworth Rotary Club, St Editha's Church, Tamworth, Tamworth and District Round Table, many businesses including Messrs E.B Hamel and Sons, Bolehall Mill, Burdetts and Faceys, Messrs Shannons; Amington Inn, Wigginton Hotel; Hopwas Church; Cooperative Society; Tamworth Soroptimist Club, Lichfield District Council; Schools in Atherstone, Atherstone Liberal Club, Atherstone Congregational Church, Atherstone Factory; Ansley Social Club, Chapel End Liberal Club and Chapel End Methodist Church, Polesworth Methodist Sunday School, Polesworth Working Men's Club and Institute, Polesworth Miners Welfare Club, Chetwynd Arms Hotel, Polesworth; Polesworth County Primary School; Dordon Sunday School, Ansley village, Wilnecote, Hurley, Mancetter, Baxterley and private individuals from all these areas."

Other news included comments from local MP Julian Snow; a request for people to offer homes to house the refugees; the offer of jobs to the migrants to work in local mines; News Sheets for the Hungarians in their own language held at Tamworth Library and the need to upgrade a hostel ready for the refugees.

"Homes for Hungarians: An Appeal to All Mining Areas" was a front page heading in the *Tamworth Herald* on December 28th

1956, written by W.E. Jones, President of the National Union of Mineworkers and W.H. Sales, Labour Member of the National Coal Board. It stated: *"There is now an opportunity to assist in the re-settlement of Hungarian refugees..."* It offered rates to be paid for lodgings to be arranged with householders. As a result, Hungarians like Gyorgy were offered a room within family homes in the Tamworth area.

The enthusiasm shown by Tamworthians and Great Britain generally was a testament to the generosity of the national spirit.

The final amount sent to the Lord Mayor of London on 1st March 1957 from Tamworth District and Rural Councils, combined with Atherstone Rural Council was an impressive £1,762.5.11 – a considerable amount in those days – raised in just three and a half months of local efforts.

THE HERALD, FRIDAY, DECEMBER, 7, 1956

AMINGTON INN RAISES £50 FOR HUNGARIAN RELIEF FUND

Customers of the Amington Inn, together with local tradespeople, collected £50 in one week-end, in aid of the Hungarian Relief Fund. And on Saturday evening a cheque for the amount was presented to the Mayor of Tamworth (Alderman E. A. Courts). The presentation was made to Mr. Courts by the manager of the Inn, Mr. Ron Starr, who, together with Mr. Syd Dennis and Mr. Albert Oliver, organised the effort. Business people in the surrounding area supported the effort by donating goods which were auctioned off on the premises.

Head Office: 14, Silver Street, Tamworth.
London Office: 80, Fleet Street; Telephone, Central 4438.
Telegrams: "Herald," Tamworth; Telephone, Tamworth 12.

FRIDAY, DECEMBER 14, 1956.

HUNGARIAN RELIEF

FURTHER CONTRIBUTIONS TO LOCAL FUNDS

MONEY continues to come in to the various local funds for Hungarian relief, and further contributions are listed below.

The Mayor of Tamworth wishes to acknowledge with thanks receipt of the following donations, which bring the total of the borough fund to date up to £566.

Acknowledged to December 7, 1955, £458 14s. 3d.; Red Lion. Bolebridge Street, £2 14s. 11d.; Lamb Inn. 3d.; Municipal Offices staff, £2 0s. 3½d.; Bolebridge Street, W.M. Club, 17s.8½d.; Anchor Inn. 13s. 9½d.; St. Chad's Church. Hopwas, £11 2s. 6d; Empire Vaults, £2 13s. 7½d.; Bricklayer's Arms, 5s. 2d.; White Horse, Lichfield Street, 2s. 7d.; Peel Arms. 12s. 4d.; Castle Hotel. 13s. 6½d.; Red Lion, Lichfield Street, 9s. 2d.; Three Tuns. 11s. 0½d.; British Legion. 6s. 8d.; Town Hall Vaults, £2 0s. 0½d.; Olivers Hotel, 11s. 8½d.; Prince of Wales, 2s. 10½d.; Civic Restaurnt. 17s.; Dog Inn. 19s. 7d.; Globe Inn. 18s. 10½d.; Kettlebrook W.M. Club, £2 10s.; Wigginton Hotel. £2 4s. 6½d.; Tamworth I.C.S. (shop. collection), £10 8s. 1d.; Grand Theatre. £11 5s. 5½d.; Mrs. Morgan, Bolebridge Street. 16s. 3½d.; Progressive W.M. Club, 9d.; Co-op. Employees' Club, 7d.; Tweedale Arms. £2 3s. 4d.; St. John's R.C. Club, 9s. 8½d.; Miners' Welfare Club. 12s. 3d.; Jolly Button Turner, £1 7s. 9d.; Townswomen's Guild, £1 1s.; Palace Theatre. £6 3s. 10d.; Methodist Circuit Youth Council, £10 17s.; Anonymous. £10 10s.; Mr. W. M. Facey, £5 5s.; Mr. S. R. Price. £2 2s.; Miss K. Lowe, £1; Miss O. Lowe, £1; Collection. Fire Station, per Mr. Goodwin. £7 3s. 6d.; Mr. W. Burdett, £2 2s.—Total to date. £566 11s.

Tamworth Rural District

The fund opened by the Chairman of the Tamworth Rural District Council (Councillor G. H. Phillips) totalled up to yesterday, £344 15s. 2d., and Councillor Phillips expresses thanks to the following:—

Previously acknowledged, £316 3s. 9d.; Wilnecote County Secondary School, £8 8s.; Members of Hurley W.M.C., £11 6s. 11d; Customers of Mr. Cooper. Anchor Inn. Hurley, 4s. 5d.; Customers of Mrs. Wright, Hurley Common. £1 1s. 5d.; Customers of Mrs. Spooner. Hurley, 6s. 10d.; Customers of Mrs. Coles. Hurley, 16s. 6d.; Collecton at Hurley. per Mrs. Pearson, £1 7s.; Collection at Hurley. per Mrs. Jones. £1 10s. 11d.; Customers of Mrs. Payne. Hurley, 5s.; Customers of Mrs. Kennings. Hurley. 2s. 4d.; Collection at Hurley. per Mr. Conway, 11s.; Customers of the White Hart Inn, Hurley. £2 11s. 2d.—Total to December 13, £344 15s. 2d.

If anyone has books in Hungarian, for which there is a great need. they are asked to hand them in to the nearest public library. when they will be forwarded to the appropriate quarter.

THE HERALD, FRIDAY, JANUARY 18, 1957

DORDON DANCE RAISES £40 FOR HUNGARIANS

A DANCE sponsored by Dordon Parish Council and organised by Mr. A. P. Rooms in aid of the Hungarian Relief Fund realised over £40 it was revealed on Thursday last week.

Mr. Rooms told the Council at their January meeting that it had been one of his most successful dances. The Chairman (Mr. W. A. Brown) extended thanks on behalf of the Council to Mr. Rooms. The money was then handed over to Mr. E. Bond, Chairman of Atherstone Rural District Council, to be added to the Chairman's fund.

The Tamworth Herald

Head Office: 14, Silver Street, Tamworth.
London Office: 80, Fleet Street; Telephone, Central 4438.
Telegrams: "Herald," Tamworth; Telephone, Tamworth 12.

FRIDAY, NOVEMBER 16, 1956.

Local funds opened for Hungarian relief

THE TRAGEDY—WHICH WAS HUNGARY

From the Mayor of Tamworth

Sir,—Once again terror, pain and death has struck at this unfortunate land. It is not my job at the moment to write of who is wrong and who is right in the invasion of Hungary, but my concern, our concern, is with the victims, especially the women and children who are now homeless and hopeless.

Those who could flee, have fled, their only possessions being the clothes they wore, going to any place away from the terror that possesses their land. There are those who could not get away, who are trying to exist in and around homes smashed by tanks, with famine and pestilence haunting them.

The Lord Mayor of London has inaugurated a fund, to be administered by the International Red Cross, to help the needs of this harassed people.

We cannot stand idly by. We must help in every way we can

Already in Tamworth there are organisations asking "What can we do?" Some will be sending cheques, and there is a move by another to hold a stall on a market day in the very near future. You will learn of that.

Now what can we do as individuals who want so dearly to help?

Parcels of clothes can be taken to the Women's Voluntary Service headquarters, next to the Market Street end of the Middle Entry, where I know the ladies will be glad to receive them.

Collections can be organised in works or factories or offices. If you have never done that before, here's a chance to learn, with sympathetic colleagues helping.

A house-to-house collection will be held. Can I have volunteers to assist?

To all members of clubs, and all in the public-houses, if you only give me for the fund the price of five cigarettes we will be getting on.

From the Chairman of Tamworth Rural District Council.

Sir,—As Chairman of Tamworth Rural District Council I have been asked by the Lord Mayor of London to make an appeal to the residents of my district for funds to help to relieve suffering by the people of Hungary, many of whom are now in sore distress and in urgent need of food, clothing and shelter.

The Red Cross is doing valiant work for Hungary but will be relying on our help to carry out their task.

I do most earnestly appeal for support as soon as possible.

Contributions should be sent to my Council's Treasurer at 92, Lichfield Street, Tamworth, who will be pleased to acknowledge same.

Cheques should be made payable to "Hungary Appeal Fund."
—G. H. PHILLIPS.

Hungarian Relief Fund

A WHIST DRIVE will be held in EDINGALE VILLAGE HALL FRIDAY, NOV. 30th, at 7-30 p.m.

Organised by Edingale and Croxall Women's Institute. (t)

ST. ANDREW'S CHURCH, CLIFTON CAMPVILLE

Clippings from local newspapers show the positive reaction of residents in the Tamworth area to the Hungarian Relief Appeal.

MINER'S HOSTEL SUGGESTED AS REFUGEE CENTRE

TAMWORTH RURAL DISTRICT COUNCIL is suggesting that the former miners' hostel at Two Gates should be used to accommodate Hungarian refugees.

The suggestion was accepted at Saturday's meeting of the Council, but the decision was criticised by Councillor Atkins, who said the hostel was not in a fit condition to house animals— let alone refugees.

Vice-chairman, Councillor Marriott replied that the hostel had been considered for housing at a time when the position was serious and he could not agree it was in such a bad state. There was a resident caretaker employed to keep the hostel in condition. He admitted that money would have to be spent to put the place in a proper state to receive the refugees and he hoped it could be put to such a use rather than remain unused.

Atherstone Rural District

The appeal made by the Chairman of Atherstone Rural District Council (Councillor E. Bond) for the Lord Mayor of London's National Hungarian and Central European Relief Fund now totals £456 14s. 8d.

Previously acknowledged, £284 14s. 11d.; Atherstone North County Junior School, £7 0s. 3d.; Polesworth Methodist Sunday School, £3 3s.; Polesworth Working Men's Club and Institute, £1 1s.; Grendon Working Men's Club and Institute, £2 2s.; Ansley Social Club and Institute, whist drives, £4 3s. 6d.; Chapel End Liberal Club, £5 5s.; Collection at Chapel End Liberal Club, £7 1s. 6d.; Sale and Son Ltd., £3 3s.; Polesworth Miners' Welfare Club, £5; St. Leonard's Church, Dordon, £4 10s. 6d.; St. Leonard's Church, Dordon, Sunday School, £1; Freasley Mission Room, £1 14s. 6d.; Chapel End Methodist Church, £6; Hartshill County Secondary School, £20 13s.; Ansley County School (second donation), 16s.; Messrs. Joseph Gillott and Sons Ltd., £1 16s.; Proceeds of a whist drive held at Church Room, Ansley Village, £12; Customers of the Chetwynd Arms Hotel, Polesworth, £1 2s.; Collection at the Regal Cinema, Atherstone, December 2 to 8, £45 5s. 6d.; Anon., £1; Arden Hill County Infants' School, £2 2s.; Atherstone Liberal Club, £5; Collection at Merevale Church, £2 7s. 8d.; Polesworth County Primary School, £3 5s.; Atherstone Congregational Church, £6 7s. 1d.; Mr. and Mrs. E. Hall, Lilac Cottage, Atherstone, £2; Collection at Hartshill Parish Church, £3 18s.; Messrs. George Ward (Barwell) Ltd., Atherstone factory, £4 5s.; Messrs. George Ward (Barwell) Ltd., Mancetter factory, £3 12s. 2d.; Methodist Church, Ridge Lane, £4 10s.; Working Men's Club, Ridge Lane, 11s. 7d.; White Hart Inn, Ridge Lane, 4s. 6d.—Total, £456 14s. 8d.

ROUND TABLE STALL

The Tamworth News & Four Shires Advertiser.

FRIDAY, NOVEMBER 23, 1956

HUNGARIAN RELIEF FUND

(Mayor of Tamworth's Appeal)

PLEASE HAND IN YOUR CONTRIBUTION TO THIS WORTHY CAUSE AT TAMWORTH ROUND TABLE'S STALL IN THE

MARKET PLACE, TAMWORTH TO-MORROW (SATURDAY)

FROM 8-30 a.m. ONWARDS

Bonehill House, Mile Oak, the NCB's hostel where refugees lived. Source: *Tamworth Herald* 2015

Homes for Hungarians
AN APPEAL TO ALL IN MINING AREAS

The following appeal to miners has been issued jointly by Mr. W. E. Jones, President of the National Union of Mineworkers, and Mr. W. H. Sales, Labour Member of the National Coal Board:—

"The tragic events in Hungary have awakened the conscience of the whole nation. People in every walk of life are anxious to know what they can do to alleviate the sufferings of the refugees who have fled from that unhappy country to seek sanctuary elsewhere.

"As always, the mineworkers of Britain have been to the fore in their expressions of solidarity and in their offers of practical help. Especially is their sympathy directed towards their fellow-miners from another country.

"There is now the opportunity to assist in the re-settlement of Hungarian refugees, and at the same time for this humanitarian operation to bring relief to our own hard-pressed industry in the form of much-needed manpower.

"The greatest single contribution which any mineworker employed by the National Coal Board can make to the success of this vitally important work is to offer accommodation in his own home to refugees from Hungary who are potential recruits to our pits."

W. E. JONES,
President—National Union of Mineworkers.

W. H. SALES,
Labour Member — National Coal Board.

If you are willing to do this please write at once, giving name, address, colliery (if applicable) and details of the accommodation you are prepared to offer, to :—

Mr. Denis Bell
Room 72, Hobart House, London, S.W.1.

or tell the nearest colliery office. The rates to be paid for lodgings will be arranged with householders.

ISSUED BY THE NATIONAL COAL BOARD, HOBART HOUSE, LONDON, S.W.1.

Homes for Hungarians: an appeal to all in mining areas. Source: The *Tamworth Herald* front-page news 28th December 1956.

England, Work & Early Years

Gyorgy continues his story...

REFUGEES FROM THE Austrian Camps were leaving to go to Sweden, Australia, the USA, Canada and other parts of the world. Offers were posted on our camp notice boards (written in Hungarian) so we could choose where to go and what jobs to do.

I liked the idea of going to Britain because it was not too far away from Hungary, which meant I could return home when communism was over. So when a job opportunity appeared on the board for coal miners in Britain, I put my name down...

Departures to England started in the winter of 1957, I think it was January. We left Austria by train, hundreds of us, all heading for different destinations in England. News of the Uprising had spread and people knew from the radio that former Hungarian Freedom Fighters were travelling through their countries. From Austria, our train passed through Germany and Belgium on its way to England.

At every station where we stopped local people came out to cheer us and to give us younger ones chocolate and gifts while cigarettes were passed to the adults. I especially remember the German people passing us sweets through the open windows and doors; more came from passengers getting on the train. They knew we were Hungarian Refugees. They were all wonderful, kind people.

After crossing the Channel we arrived in London, where we stayed for a few days, after which we were sent to Stoke on Trent to a miners' hostel. We stayed there for a few weeks until the National Coal Board found us work at different pits all over the country. Twenty-seven of us, all males, were sent to Tamworth, Staffordshire, to work at Birch Coppice Colliery.

We lived in Bone Hill House, which was a miners' hostel at that time, owned by the National Coal Board. We underwent training at Wood End, where the Coal Board had apprenticeships for miners, then went to work at Birch Coppice Mine. We worked as miners for a while until the Mine Workers Union decided that foreign workers were not acceptable down the pit. That finished us as coal miners.

I was the youngest lad in the hostel and didn't talk about the Uprising. I tried to forget it. Even if I had tried to tell anyone what had happened, nobody would have believed a 14-year-old. So nobody in the hostel knew anything about my experiences, nor did the other refugees share their stories. They hadn't been freedom fighters, they just wanted to leave Hungary for a better life, knowing that the country was condemned to years of Soviet rule. They just wanted to get out while they could.

HUNGARIANS ROCK 'N ROLL

WHEN in Britain do as the British do, believe 27 Hungarian refugees living in a N.C.B. hostel at Wilnecote, and so when members of the Wilnecote Youth Club invited them to a dance on Tuesday, the stately dances of Vienna were forgotten in favour of Rock 'n' Roll.

Arriving eight weeks ago to learn English, the Hungarian boys, whose ages are between 15 and 17, had no contacts outside the hostel and received only a few letters from home. Most of their time was taken up with lessons and playing amongst themselves in the games room.

But Miss Price Evans, the Tamworth youth officer, had a better idea. With the help of Captain Oxton, the Wilnecote Youth Club leader, Councillor Mrs. Bennett, a member of the Wilnecote management committee, and Mr. T. Kennedy, of Tamworth Youth Club, girls were chosen from both youth clubs to visit the hostel on Thursday, March 7.

In spite of the language barrier the evening was a great success, and a return by the boys to the Wilnecote Youth Club planned for Tuesday.

Not to be outdone by the girls, several boys from the Youth Club arrived on Tuesday, and in the course of the evening England challenged Hungary to a football match, a boxing bout and a games evening, which will be held in three weeks' time.

Once again the evening was a great success and laughter flowed freely as Hungarian goulash until 11 o'clock.

The aim of the Wilnecote and Tamworth youth clubs is that more clubs should invite the Hungarians to spend an evening with them and that families should ask them to tea or to watch the television.

Said Mrs. Bennett: "They are boys who have suddenly had to become men; now we must teach them to be boys again."

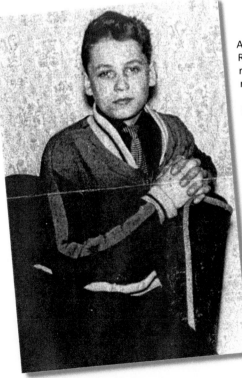

A report on the Hungarian Rock 'n' Roll night organised in support of the refugees showing Gyorgy in the front row on the far right.

Source: *Tamworth Herald* 15th March 1957

Gyorgy, aged 14½ years, ready to go to the Hungarian Rock 'n' Roll night. Taken at Bonehill House, Mile Oak, where he and other refugees were living at the time.

We stayed at Bonehill House for about six months and made friends with some of the Tamworth lads and other local people. A man came to the house to help us settle in; I am not sure whether he was a teacher or someone from the Coal Board sent to help us. He taught us a little English. We didn't attend a school in Britain when we first arrived, so I expect this was a kind of introduction to our new lives.

Another man came from Social Services and got me into lodgings with an English family. I now learned the language a lot quicker because I had to in order to communicate with the family.

The local community was very welcoming and even organised a 'Rock & Roll Night' to introduce us to the area, held at Wilnecote Youth Club in March 1957 (see opposite).

We Hungarians had a few ups and downs before the British girls took to us. I guess they were nervous because we were foreigners but when we started to attend Tamworth Youth Club in Albert Road they were able to get to know us and realise that we weren't so different. For me it was a good incentive to learn to speak English better in order to talk to the girls. The English lads were a bit jealous at first but it all came right in the end and we all became friends.

None of them knew that I had been a freedom fighter. I never talked about it with my new British friends. I was very young and it had been a hellish experience, seeing people dead in the streets and wondering whose mother or father had been killed.

While I was at Bonehill House the other Hungarians and I often went swimming. Mrs Bennett,[1] a local councillor from

Amington, had introduced us to the popular open-air swimming baths in the Castle Grounds at Tamworth. One day during that summer I was at the swimming baths in Mrs Bennett's company as she was talking to a local couple called Mr and Mrs Perry, who had brought their children, Julia and Andrew to go swimming. (Julia later became Julia Pinner, the author of this book).

Mrs Bennett introduced me saying, "This is Gyorgy from Hungary, who did very brave things in the Hungarian Uprising."

Mrs Perry told me this story many years later. I did not remember any of it, as I had only been in Britain for about four months at the time and would not have understood what was being said.

But I must have picked up the language quite quickly because I used to translate for the rest of the Hungarian lads. I think that I learned English quickest because I was underage and had to be placed in lodgings with English families where I picked up the language a lot faster. I had to, since nobody in England understood a word of Hungarian.

I also taught myself to write English. Whenever I understood what a word meant I copied how it was written from books or newspapers. It was hard and I made mistakes but I slowly got better.

After the Union decided that no Hungarians were to be allowed to work down the pit most of the Hungarians left Tamworth to find work elsewhere in the country, leaving just four of us. We all found work and Bonehill House reverted to its former use, whatever that had been.

I went into lodgings with a family at Fazely, and started working at Foseco. Later I

---

[1] Mrs Bennett was known locally as Chick Webb (her maiden name).

moved lodgings to Gillway and worked in a garage as an apprentice mechanic at a place called Ford & Rowley, when I was about 16 or 17 years old. Mr Rowley was a wonderful boss and the other workmen were also great. However, sometimes the younger ones would ask me to go to Mr Rowley with a message, telling me what words to use. These were swear words, of course! I didn't know because I had only learned a few English phrases at the camp in Austria such as "thank-you" and "good morning" plus a few more at the Miners Hostel.

The boss realised what was going on and said "Gyorgy, those are bad words!" This made me determined to learn better English.

Not long after that, one of the boys came to me and said "Go and tell Mr Rowley to..." and I was able to say "You go and tell him yourself!"

From that day on the teasing stopped and we got on really well because they knew I was onto their little game.

When Ford & Rowley closed down I moved on to other places. I was employed at a bus garage called Midland Red (now Arriva) in Tamworth for a few weeks before going to Mile Oak Garage, run by the three Jackson Brothers.

I had several different lodgings in Tamworth, some good, some not so good. I also had several other jobs; I worked at Alders Paper Mills, I was a bricklayer's labourer, a fabricator's labourer. Finally I became a coalman delivering sacks of coal around the Midlands and I was to do this for almost ten years. (See next chapter).

During this time I had been writing letters to my Mum and sister and when I had a job

and could afford the stamps I also sent some parcels for my mother.

By now it was 1966 and I was 23 years old. At this time I met a self-employed lorry driver called John Pinner, aged 26 and also a coalman, delivering bag coal locally.

By this time I was married and my wife Sylvia was a hair stylist who worked at a Hairdressing Salon in Tamworth town centre called *Brenda's* along with another stylist called Julia Perry.

Sylvia thought that Julia and John would get on well so we arranged a blind date for them, to meet up at our flat in Dordon in July 1967. I had to go and fetch John because he was shy, and persuade him to come and meet Julia!

Sylvia was right, they certainly did get on well. Their wedding took place on 30th March 1968 and John asked me to be his Best Man! We have kept in touch ever since and Julia helped me write this book.

Before the wedding, John took me to meet his parents in Erdington. As he introduced me to his Mum he said, "This is my pal Gyorgy who's from Hungary."

The next minute Mrs Pinner presented me with a plate of cheese on toast, saying, "Are you hungry my lad?" She had misheard what John had said but I was not complaining – it was very tasty snack!

John and Julia had daughters and if I saw them out with friends I would have a chat. Their pals would ask "who is he?" and they would reply, "It was Gyorgy who got our Mum and Dad together. If it wasn't for him we wouldn't be here!"

Work and Family

ONE DAY THE Transport Manager at the National Coal Board where I was employed, asked me if I would like to work for myself: they would provide the sacks, scales and weights but I would need to get myself a lorry. There was a man working for the Coal Board in the offices called Ray Fretter; I had a word with him about setting up in business on my own. He listened and said that he would help me with the business: he loaned me the money and I brought an old second hand lorry. We started to work for ourselves!

We named the company "Frenad Coal and Haulage" which were the first three letters of both of our surnames, Fretter and Nadasdy. It was difficult to start off in business on your own, because you had to have an Operators Licence off the Ministry of Transport. I attended several court hearings in Birmingham but there were always objectors to the licence being given, such as British Rail, British Road Services and local operators. We started with a "C" licence, went onto a restricted "B" then finally a restricted "C" licence. (Restricted means you can only carry your own goods such as coal or the company that you worked for, not from any outside company)

I spent 27 days in one year at the hearings. On the last day, a gentleman on the board said

"You are so determined and enthusiastic that I will give you an Open International Licence, called and "Open A" so that you can do any other jobs in Great Britain or in Europe.

It was like a dream come true! For the first five years I worked for The National Coal Board, employing a driver's mate. It was good working for the National Coal Board, sub contracting from them. Come rain or shine, we fulfilled our contract.

The coal hauling contract finished in the 1970's and I said goodbye to my driver's mate; I thanked him for all that he had done for me. He soon got another job as a tipper lorry driver, because in those days you could get a job straight away.

I then started with a company called Wilnecote Brick. All the lorries working for them were loaded by hand as there weren't any forklift trucks. Two labourers from the company and I used to load the lorry ourselves. When we delivered the bricks to the sites, the bricklayer's labourers and I had to offload the lorry by hand between us.

About this time I was in my last lodgings in Borough Road, Tamworth. I befriended the local lads and played football for the team called Borough Park Rovers. I had played football for a lot of local teams in the past, in this area.

From work I used to see two of the local lads whom I played football with, who worked in a butcher's shop. On the opposite side of the road was a dress shop and above it was a Ladies Hairdressing Salon called "Brenda's:" four or five girls worked there. Sometimes they came to the window and looking down, they could see me there. They went over to the butchers shop and kept asking my friend Malcolm "Who is he?" He said that I was his mate, living in the borough, and that I was Hungarian. After five days, Malcolm told me that the girls had been asking about me, and that they liked the look of me! There was one young lady called Sylvia who used to tell her friends "If he asks me I will marry him!" Malcolm told me this and a few weeks later I met the young lady; I started seeing her: this was in 1966.

I liked Sylvia very much and eventually met her parents. She told her mum and dad that I would like to marry her. Sylvia's dad was not impressed and she told this to her brother and sister. Sylvia's mum told her dad," The lad is alright; he has no family here. He must have had a very poor life" Whatever my mother in law said on my behalf worked, because five months later they agreed to let us marry on 8th April, 1967, in Saint Editha's Church, Tamworth.

There wasn't any family here for me, so my business partner was my best man. We lived in a flat for eight months above a Chemist Shop in Dordon. Later on we purchased a little terraced house that cost us £1,100, in the same street as my friend, Ray Fretter. The little house was good, with a garden where I used to grow vegetables. I soon made friends with the neighbours and locals. Dordon was a mining village where everyone knew each other. We went to Dordon Working Man's Club where they held annual garden shows where vegetables such as onions, leeks and beans were displayed and flowers such as sweet peas, dahlias, chrysanthemums and many other items were on show.

Everyone used to love this annual show, which was actually Dordon's Horticultural Society. Two years later they asked me if I would like to be their secretary and I accepted the role. I became a very good gardener: you had to be because nearly all the villages surrounding Dordon were mining villages and they all knew their onions!

It was a tight community with many coal board houses, all with large gardens so of course, we all made use of them, growing vegetables in the back garden. In those days there weren't any superstores, just village shops, corner shops, village post offices that only sold what was essential. There was also the milkman, postman, bread man and coalman delivering to the houses so we all knew what to expect and where to go to buy what we needed.

Gyorgy and Sylvia's wedding at St Editha's Church in Tamworth on 8th April 1967.

Our Babies

Sylvia became pregnant in 1970 and on 4th October gave birth to a baby girl. She was so lovely, we named her Luci Anna and asked Ray to be her godfather. He loved her to bits.

When Luci was about two, Ray said, "Why don't you sell your house and move in with me?" His house was huge and he lived on his own. After much discussion we agreed to move in with him.

While staying there we were able to save some money and eventually we had enough saved to buy a house which had previously belonged to Sylvia's Aunty. We moved in, settled down and started a new life, getting to know our neighbours. Ray used to visit us there. Sadly, just two years later, he died.

Some time later Sylvia gave birth to a baby boy who tragically died at birth. We never even saw him, which upset us both very much. It would have been so good for Luci to have had a little brother, but sadly this was not to be.

A few years later, on 13th March 1981, Sylvia gave birth to a little girl who we called Laura. She was gorgeous and Luci adored her. My wife was wonderful and looked after both our daughters really well.

Luci used to come with me in the lorry sometimes. There weren't any sleeper cabs back then, so I used to strap her into the passenger seat. She loved those trips out. I used to get up early in the morning and she would hear the floorboards creak and jump out of bed, shouting, "Daddy, Daddy, I'm coming!"

Sylvia would get her ready and then we would go off trucking together. We stopped at transport cafés where she would say, "Egg and chips Daddy!"

All this time my family in Hungary did not see either of my girls, except in the photographs I sent them with my letters home.

Our London Nightmare

ONE DAY RAY asked if Sylvia and I would like to go to London for a sightseeing weekend and we accepted his invitation. It would be a real treat... Or so we thought.

So it was that we set off for our weekend in London early in March 1968. We would be staying at the Regent Palace Hotel. Sylvia wanted to go to St. James's Park to feed the ducks and afterwards we went for a stroll. Unfortunately, we became separated in the London traffic.

We had previously agreed that under such circumstances we would meet at Trafalgar Square, which we thought would be a large open space where we would be able to find each other.

I made my way to Trafalgar Square and found a spot where I thought I would be clearly visible to Sylvia and Ray when they turned up.

As I stood there, minding my own business, I noticed a large crowd of people who appeared to be holding some kind of demonstration. There were also quite a lot of policemen.

The next thing I knew, I was approached by two police officers.

"Move!" said one of them. "You're causing an obstruction.."

"I'm sorry," I said. "I can't go, or I won't be able to find my wife."

"Move!" He repeated. "You are obstructing the footpath!"

"Haven't you got anything better to do?" I asked him.

He seemed to take exception to this comment because the next thing I knew I was being bundled into a police car and taken to Cannon Row police station, where I was charged with being a demonstrator and causing an obstruction. This in spite of the fact that I was simply standing there and was at least 200 yards from where the demonstration was taking place.

Sylvia, who had been on the other side of the road at the time, had witnessed the whole incident. She saw the two policemen bundling me into a police car and managed to reach us just in time before they drove off with me, but they refused to tell her either what I was supposed to have done or where they were taking me.

Quite naturally she felt scared to be suddenly stranded there all alone and as I drove away in the back of the police car I was worried about her. Fortunately she spoke to some other policeman and a little later and they suggested that she should go to Cannon Row police station. She waited

EX-REFUGEE MR. NADASDY TELLS OF NIGHTMARE TRIP

Mercury Staff Reporter

A WEEKEND special treat, sightseeing in London, became a nightmare for a Midland couple, Mr. George Nadasdy and his wife, Sylvia.

A pleasant after-lunch stroll through the streets of the West End to Trafalgar Square ended in tears and trouble.

Mr. and Mrs. Nadasdy, from Dordon, near Tamworth, were parted by the crowds. Their simple re-union plan led to:

- The husband being hustled off in a police van.
- The wife being stranded, not knowing where her husband was being taken.
- The cost of the trip going up by £20.

Demonstration

So that they could spot each other, the plan was for them to stay in open ground away from other people. But in the distance was a C.N.D. anti-Vietnam war demonstration.

While Mr. Nadasdy was standing on the pavement looking for his wife, two policemen hustled him off and charged him with obstruction. But the follow-

Shock end to that weekend in London

ing day the charge against him was dismissed.

Last night Mr. Nadasdy, a 25-year-old Hungarian refugee, said: "I do not want to have anything to do with demonstrations of any sort. I had enough of them in Hungary before I came here. I would not get mixed up with anything like that.

A shock

"I think it is a pity that in a country like this a man can be dragged off when he has done no harm to any-one. It was a shock, and I did not know where my wife was for some time.

"On the other hand, I can see the police point of view — especially after the terrible trouble they had to undergo on the previous Sunday."

Explaining what happened, Mr. Nadasdy, who is joint-owner of a lorry, said: "Neither my wife nor I know London. We were having a good look around. We were going to look at the ducks in St. James's Park but got separated by the traffic in Trafalgar Square.

"We arranged beforehand that if we lost contact we would stay in the same area, not wander away, but find a clear space where we would be visible.

'Sorry'

"In the distance I could see this anti-Vietnam war demonstration. They were at least 200 yards away. I was in a clear space well away from them.

"Then a policeman came up and said: 'Move. You are causing an obstruction.'

"I said: 'I am sorry, I cannot go, otherwise I shall

Mr. and Mrs. Nadasdy

not be able to find my wife again.'

"He said: 'Move. You are obstructing the footpath.'

"I told the policeman: 'Haven't you got anything better to do?

"Two policemen then came along and took me off to Cannon Row Police Station."

Scared

Mrs. Sylvia Nadasdy added: "The incident scared me. I was over the other side of the road. I saw George in a clear space then he had gone.

"I saw two policemen putting him into a police car and I managed to reach them. They would not tell me what he had done nor where he was being taken. I did not know what to do.

"Later, I saw some other policemen and they suggested I went to Cannon Row Police Station. I waited while George was bailed to appear at court on the following day.

"It cost us a lot of money because we lost time from work and had to travel to London all over again. We reckon it cost us at least an extra £20."

Mr. Nadasdy added: "After

the case was dismissed, a police inspector came up, but he did not apologise. He said if I had any complaint I was to write to New Scotland Yard.

"The magistrate told me that I would have to pick the right weekend before we go to London again. But that will not be for a long time."

● Editorial comment: P. 10

The *Tamworth Herald* reports on Gyorgy and Sylvia's nightmare trip to London in March 1968.

there whilst I was bailed to appear in court the following day.

The whole incident cost us a lot of money because we both lost time from work and had to travel to London all over again on Monday in order for me to appear in court.

We reckoned that this cost us at least an extra £20. In 1968 that was about two weeks of an average wage.

At the court hearing, I said that I wanted nothing to do with demonstrations of any sort. I'd had enough of them in Hungary before coming to England. I would not get mixed up with anything like that.

I said that I could see the police point of view, especially as there had been trouble during the demonstrations caused by hooligans engaging in violence, which needed to be dealt with, but I also said that it was a pity that, in a great country like this, a man could be dragged off the street by the police when he was doing no harm to anyone. I was not behaving like a thug. I also said that as my wife watched the scene unfold it had caused her much distress and alarm, during what should have been an enjoyable stay in the city.

The court acquitted me that Monday. Afterwards a police inspector came up to me but did not apologise. He just said that if I had any complaint, I would have to write to New Scotland Yard. The magistrate told me that next time I returned to London, to make sure that I picked the right weekend. I said "That will not happen for a long time!"

My experience was reported in the Press. Our local newspaper report is shown opposite.

A national newspaper also ran the story under the heading 'Justice in the Rough':

"Everyone makes mistakes. The politicians do. Journalists do. And so do the police. Some mistakes are more costly than others. Some are more culpable. Some are more honest errors. Some are caused by foolishness, a lack of foresight or just faulty judgment.

All ought to have one thing in common: as soon as the mistake is discovered the guilty should do everything possible to make amends to the innocent victim... Naturally his wife was alarmed to see this happen when she strolled along to meet him. She and her husband were put to some inconvenience – not to mention distress – before he was acquitted the following day.

The police had made a mistake; a silly one but forgivable in the circumstances. For a Vietnam peace demonstration was taking place in Trafalgar Square while Mr Nadasdy was waiting. After the ugly scenes in the West End the previous Sunday, the police were naturally on the alert for trouble and who can blame them? The stresses of the moment may excuse the police action, but they do not justify it.

What makes the offence worse is that no attempt has been made to reimburse Mr Nadasdy for the expense he incurred in establishing his innocence. Nor has he any representative of the police visited him to apologise for the mistake.

At best this is a bad public relations. At worst it shows a deplorable disregard for the human decencies on which our society is founded. Mr Nadasdy is entitled to complain that justice is rough."

HOME OFFICE
Lunar House Wellesley Road Croydon CR9 2BY

Telephone 01-681 3421

MESSRS. PICKERING & PICKERING,
SOLS.
9, COLEHILL,
TAMWORTH
STAFFORDSHIRE

Please reply to The Under Secretary of State
Your reference BWB/JM/1517

Our reference N124311

Date 30/4/81

Dear Sirs

I am writing in reply to your letter of 10 APRIL 1981 about the application made by MR G. NADASDY for the grant of a certificate of naturalisation.

Applications for naturalisation are decided at the discretion of the Home Secretary and extensive enquiries are therefore made into every application. These enquiries, which include an interview with the applicant take many months to complete and in order to be fair to everyone applications are dealt with strictly in the order in which they are received.

I am afraid that because of the necessary economies in staffing and heavy arrears of work at every stage of the processing, it is at present taking several months before we can examine an application in order to decide whether it should be sent out for the usual full enquiries, and it will be some considerable time yet before we are able to deal with applications as quickly as we would like. I can assure you, however, that if your client's application proceeds to the enquiry stage there will be no avoidable delay in letting you have a decision when the enquiries have been completed and we have been able to give your client's application final consideration. In the meanwhile, however, we cannot undertake to answer further enquiries regarding the progress of your client's application.

Yours faithfully

P. Canovan

P CANOVAN

Letter from the Home Office regarding my application for British Citizenship in 1981.

British Citizenship and My Return to Hungary

I DIDN'T DARE TO go back home to Hungary until I had a British passport but unfortunately it took me 25 years to get one! It took such a long time because first I needed to become a British citizen.

Mr Titterton, a neighbour of mine in Glascote Heath, was a Justice of the Peace and was kind enough to support my application to become a British citizen. He signed all the paperwork but I needed another signature from someone who had known me for a long time. As I had known John Pinner since 1966, as a friend and work colleague, I asked him if he would be prepared to help. John gladly agreed and came to our house at Engine Lane, Glascote to sign the documentation.

My Alsatian dog, William, was eating his dinner in our yard and snarled at John as he came through the gate.

"William... don't you dare!" said John – but unfortunately William DID dare – and bit John on his backside! Fortunately, John still agreed to sign the paperwork!

This enabled me to apply, at last, for a British Passport and in due course I was finally awarded one.

I hadn't seen my family for 25 years and they hadn't ever met my wife or children (although they had seen photos, which I had sent to them by post). This was the first opportunity, in 1982, for us all to go and visit them. I was really excited and I bought an old Ford Thames Campervan to take us there. Sylvia's dad took one look at it and said, "You won't even get out of Tamworth in that old thing!"

However, I proved him wrong. I fixed it up and we went on to make the trip to Hungary and back TWICE in that same van!

We travelled through France, Belgium, Germany and Austria and arrived at the Hungarian border. The border guard looked at our passports and then took me into a very dark room, with windows that couldn't be seen through, to ask me the purpose of my visit. I replied that I had come to see my family, that they had never met my wife and children and had only seen photos that we had sent.

They kept me there for what seemed a long time, but may have been just an hour. Because I had left Hungary just after the revolution, I suppose he was suspicious. In 1982 Hungary was still under Communist rule. I told Sylvia before I went with the guard that if anything happened she should get in touch with the British Embassy in Hungary, although I was fairly confident that they couldn't touch me because I had a British passport. Nevertheless, they still kept me there for a bit longer than they should have done, asking me many questions, such as, "Why have you come back here and where are you going?" and "Why did you leave Hungary in 1956?" Every now and then they would leave the room and I could hear them talking outside. Of course I didn't tell them I had been a freedom fighter; I just said that I had just left as a 14 year old. Fortunately, there was no paperwork about me for them to check up on, so they eventually had to let me go.

It had been a nerve-racking experience but, with sighs of relief, we were now able to drive on towards Budapest, where we finally arrived at the apartment block where my mother lived on the first floor. The caretaker let me in via the main entrance. I climbed the stairs and nervously rang the doorbell.

Mum opened the door, looked at me, and said, "Who are you?"

"I am your son!" I said.

When she realised who I was, she burst into tears. This was just seconds before she saw Sylvia and her grandchildren, who she hugged affectionately. Mum was so excited to see us all. Sylvia was also emotional, as it was the first time she had met her mother-in-law. Of course I had sent letters from England with photos of Sylvia and the girls, plus some British paper cash (letters weren't scanned in those days). I knew she had received the letters but wondered if all the money had got through to her.

After our emotional reunion, we settled in for the stay with Mum.

Later on during that stay we went to see my younger brother Pali (who was just two years my junior) and his wife and daughter, who lived in another street not far from my mother. Sylvia asked if the toilet was upstairs. "No," was the reply. "It's at the bottom of the garden!" It was a shared, non-flushing toilet with a wooden seat type of arrangement over a dug-out latrine! Things in Hungary were still quite different from Britain, even in the 1980s. You could see women washing in the streams of little villages near the river Danube, as they had done for centuries.

The next day we all went to see my sister Nusi and her son Janchi and his children. We were all so excited; it was great to see them after all this time. They were all very welcoming to Sylvia and our children, who loved the whole experience. It was wonderful; a dream come true for us all.

Back home in Budapest at last! Pictured from left to right: daughter Luci, Gyorgy, daughter Laura, wife Sylvia, sister Nusi and brother Pisti in 1982.

Surprise! Surprise! with Cilla Black

AS I MENTIONED in an earlier chapter, I knew that my older brother Peter had emigrated to Australia after the uprising in 1956 but unfortunately we had lost touch and I did not know where in Australia he lived.

In 1984 a new show called *Surprise Surprise* had just started on ITV. Hosted by Cilla Black, it was broadcast on Sunday evenings and, among other things, the show's format involved finding long-lost friends or relatives and reuniting them live on TV.

Unknown to me, in 1985 Sylvia wrote to the programme to ask if they could find my brother Peter.

I think it was the Red Cross who actually found him; he was living in Melbourne.

The show's researchers phoned Sylvia to tell her the news and they secretly arranged for a reunion between Peter and I to take place live on TV.

On the appointed day, of course, we had to be at the TV studio where the programme was made, so in order that I wouldn't suspect anything, Sylvia gave me the cover story that she had written to the show on her own behalf and that they were going to reunite her with an old friend of hers.

We took the children along with us. Our eldest daughter Lucy loved staying in a

hotel in London. Laura was too young to be on the set with us, so she had to stay in the studios, where she was well looked after.

We were led to our seats at the end of a row (for easy access to the set, I realised afterwards) and settled in to watch the show. I thought that I was just going to be a spectator, so naturally I felt shocked and nervous when Cilla called me forward onto the set.

To my great surprise and delight Kay Kerzmane (our English teacher from at the refugee camp in Austria in 1956) was brought onto the set. She and her family had been so kind to me and I was able to thank her for the time she had spent teaching me some basic English words and for the kindness she shown when she invited me to spend Christmas with her family in Vienna.

Kay explained to Cilla that it had been a grim time for the youngest refugees like me, whose lives and schooling had been interrupted. English classes were given to those who wanted to emigrate to the UK, the United States or Australia. There were many official forms to complete, so the refugees needed help with these too.

She explained that Peter and I had been at different camps and had not known of each other's presence. Peter had chosen to migrate to Australia and I to England and

Surprise Surprise! February 1986
Gyorgy has no idea that Cilla is about
to call him and Sylvia on stage.

Cilla introduces Kay Kerzmane, who
taught English to the Hungarians in
the Austrian Refugee camp.

Cilla reveals that Peter has been flown
from Australia to meet Gyorgy and
there follows an emotional reunion
for the two brothers, thirty years
since last seeing each other.

Gyorgy is emotional and the two brothers look at each other as if they cannot quite believe what is happening.

Cilla closes the show as Gyorgy and Peter continue to gaze at each other in contentment and disbelief.

All photos: CB Prime Ltd.

thus we had been separated and we hadn't seen each other for 30 years.

Of course the big surprise of the evening was when Peter was brought on to the set. I was over the moon and so thankful for what Sylvia had done for me. To meet my brother and Kay on this programme was just fantastic and Cilla Black was brilliant! Both during and after the show she was so re-assuring, friendly and natural with us; it was like talking to a friend. She was just a wonderful lady. I couldn't thank her enough and told her so after the programme. She said that I was one of the few who actually said thank-you.

Peter came to stay with us for two weeks after the show, which gave us chance to get to know one another again. We did not talk about the Uprising at the time because we didn't want those memories brought back. We talked about work and our life experiences, about both good and bad things. We enjoyed a drink together.

Peter was so excited to meet up with us and to visit England for the first time. Before he returned to Australia, he stayed in London for a while.

We agreed to keep in touch and write to each other, now that I knew where he lived.

I still 'phone him about twice a month in the early morning (because of the time difference between here and Melbourne). We also met up in Hungary for the 50th Anniversary of the Uprising, which is covered in the next chapter.

A photo taken by Peter in Budapest in 2006 during the 50th Anniversary of the Hungarian Uprising showing Gyorgy next to the statue of a young freedom fighter called Janchi in Corvin Ter.

The 50ᵗʰ Anniversary, 2006

MY BROTHER PETER and I had an invitation from Jozsef Szarvas, the head of the Hungarian Freedom Fighters Association of the United Kingdom, based in Surrey, to return to Hungary for the 50ᵗʰ Anniversary of the uprising on 23ʳᵈ October 2006. The 23ʳᵈ October (this was the first day of the Uprising in 1956) was declared a national holiday after the inauguration of the Third Hungarian Republic in 1989.

Peter would be coming all the way from Australia, so we arranged to meet in Hungary. Unfortunately, there was conflict within the Hungarian government at that time and the 50ᵗʰ Anniversary was spoiled because of it.

The celebration was to be held in Parliament Square but when we arrived there the officials wouldn't let us in because the government was expecting trouble. The square was fenced off and only a few select people were allowed in.

My brother and I were not among them, even though we had official invitations. Naturally we were very disappointed. Peter had travelled all the way from Australia and I had from England. We were devastated.

We had been eagerly looking forward to this celebration of the historical events in which we had participated as young men, leading both of us to live in exile for the rest of our lives. But it was not to be.

I stayed in Hungary for a week. At least I got to spend some time with my family there. I also visited the Hungarian Army Museum, where I saw the famous photograph of myself, aged fourteen, as a Freedom Fighter, presumably on display due to the 50ᵗʰ Anniversary. When I returned some years later, it had been replaced by other items.

On page 155 of the book *IGAZSAGOT '56-NAK* there is a photo of me that Peter took during the 50ᵗʰ Anniversary in which I am seen showing my photo from 1956 to other people at the event.

Later Peter and I visited Corvin ter, where he took a photo of me standing by a statue of a young boy called Janchi who was killed in the Uprising. He was one of the youngest Freedom Fighters, only 12 years of age when killed. People had placed wreaths and flowers in his memory (see photo opposite).

The following pages contain a few accounts of the 50ᵗʰ Anniversary of the Uprising that tell the story of what happened.[1]

Demonstrators clash with police

Demonstrators clashed with police this week in Budapest on the 50ᵗʰ Anniversary of Hungary's uprising against Soviet

---

[1] *Voice of America* website (voanews.com).

Magyar Szabadságharcos Szövetség az Egyesült Királyságban
Alapítva 1957-ben
Elnök : Szarvas József
27 Aragon Ave Thames Ditton Surrey KT7 0PY.
Tel : 0044-208-398 1541
E-mail : joe @szarvas.demon.co.uk

Nádasdy György bajtársnak

Tamworth
Staffs

2006 július 24

Kedves Gyuri !

Itt küldöm az igért programot az évfordulóra.
Örömmel venném, ha belépnél sorainkba. Szükséges lenne,
hogy egy pár sorban megínád életrajzodat napjainkig,
kezdve, hogy hol születtél és hol voltál.
mit csináltál 56-ban.

Várom válaszodat   időközben a legjobbakat,
Bajtársi üdvözlettel,

Szarvas József s.k.

Dear Gyuri

I send here the promised anniversary programme. You would be welcome to enter our ranks. It would be necessary to send a few words back today about your biography, from where you were born and where you were in 1956.
Generally what it was in '56.
I am waiting and looking forward to your best reply in the meantime

Fraternal Regards

József Szarvas s k

Official letter inviting Gyorgy to attend the 50th Anniversary of the Hungarian Uprising in Budapest, 2006.

domination. But this time they are protesting the Socialist government's economic policies and fact that current Prime Minister Ferenc Gyurcsany lied about the dire economic situation of the country to win re-election earlier this year...

Eighty-one-year-old Hungarian journalist Andras Biro was a witness to those events, which began on October 23rd in Budapest's Bem Square where thousands of students gathered to hear the list of demands for reform by Hungary's Communist government.

Although Hungary is a free country today, the ruling Socialist Party and the right-wing opposition Fidesz are struggling for dominance. And, as Andras Biro says, on the 50th Anniversary of the 1956 uprising, each one of them tries to portray the event as "closer to its own philosophy."

Hungary Commemorates 1956 Revolution Amid Political Tensions

The president of Hungary has appealed for unity among Hungarians as anti-government protests threaten to overshadow the 50th Anniversary of the Hungarian Revolution against Soviet rule.

Many elderly Hungarians still remember the shots that reverberated through the streets – and were heard on the airwaves – as fighting broke out near the radio station in central Budapest. Freedom fighters tried to keep control of the station by holding off the much better armed Communist forces.

The radio station was a crucial information tool during the 1956 Revolution against Soviet rule and Hungary's Moscow-backed government. But the struggle for freedom that began October 23, 1956 was crushed less than two weeks later by Soviet forces.

About 2,800 Hungarians died in the fighting and 200,000 others fled to the West.

Now 50 years later, Hungary is free, the Soviet Union is an ever-fading memory, and yet tensions are again high in the country, this time sparked by the anniversary celebrations.

On Sunday, during an awards ceremony in the parliament building, several former freedom fighters refused to shake hands with Socialist Prime Minister Ferenc Gyurcsany. Mr. Gyurcsany was born five years after the revolution, but he was a leader of Hungary's Communist youth movement in the 1980's, and recently admitted he lied to voters about the economy to win re-election. Outside the parliament building people shouted for his resignation.

The ceremonies to mark the anniversary began Sunday with a concert at the Hungarian State Opera. Just before the performance began, one of the foreign leaders who are in Budapest to mark the anniversary, Austrian President Heinz Fischer, urged Hungarians to overcome their divisions and to celebrate the lasting importance of the revolution 50 years ago.

"One thing is clear, the freedom fight of 1956 was not in vain as it showed the courage of the Hungarian people," said Heinz Fischer. He added that the Soviet military was in fact the moral loser. What was bloodily crushed in 1956, Mr. Fischer said, was achieved peacefully in 1989.

Ceremonies Monday to mark the anniversary includes the unveiling of a new monument in Budapest's Heroes' Square to honour those who died in the uprising 50 years ago.

Hungarian PM Blames Opposition for Budapest Rioting

Hungarian Prime Minister Ferenc Gyurcsany has blamed the right-wing opposition for riots in Budapest Monday that marred celebrations marking the 50th Anniversary of the country's 1956 revolt against Soviet rule. In an address to parliament Tuesday, the socialist prime minister accused conservative opposition leader and former Prime Minister Viktor Orban of inciting extremists with inflammatory language. For its part, Mr. Orban's Fidesz party again called for the prime minister's resignation because of alleged excessive force by police trying to quell the rioting.

Police used tear gas, water cannon and rubber bullets against hundreds of protesters in violence that left 167 people injured. Police also reported detaining 131 people. Protesters have demanded that Mr. Gyurcsany resign. The protests started last month after he was heard on a leaked audiotape admitting that he lied repeatedly about the state of the country's economy in order to win re-election.

Violence Overshadows Hungary's 1956 Revolution Commemoration

Street riots and anti-government demonstrations have overshadowed the 50th Anniversary of Hungary's 1956 Revolution against Soviet rule. The arrival of presidents, prime ministers and royals from different countries did not ease tensions.

Riot police fired rubber bullets and tear gas at anti-government protesters near the parliament building. Hungarian demonstrators even gained control of a Soviet-era tank, which had been parked in Budapest as part of the 50th Anniversary commemorations of the 1956 Revolution against Soviet rule. Dozens of people were injured in the fighting.

The protesters are angry because, they say, Communists have returned to power. Hungarian Prime Minister Ferenc Gyurcsany was leader of the Communist youth movement. The demonstrators are also furious that he has admitted to lying about the dire economic situation of the country in order to win re-election this year.

Hungary's main right-wing opposition party Fidesz boycotted official ceremonies Monday, holding instead its own rally that drew as many as 100,000 people. Among them, Wilfried Martens, president of the European People's Party, the largest within the European Union. He told the crowd that only Prime Minister Ferenc Gyurcsany is responsible for the current tensions in Hungary.

"The present Hungarian upheaval is caused by one man," said Wilfried Martens.

The opposition rally, combined with the riots, overshadowed government events designed to mark the anniversary of the failed revolt that sealed Hungary's fate as a Soviet satellite state until the fall of the Iron Curtain in 1989.

In front of the Hungarian parliament building, the Socialist-led government tried to hold commemorations with dignitaries, including presidents, prime ministers and royals. As riot police looked on, a military band tried to outdo those shouting slogans against the government. Officials from around the world placed white roses at the foot of a marble monument commemorating those who died in the failed revolution.

The fight for freedom, democracy and independence from the Soviet Union began October 23, but after initial optimism, the revolt was crushed by Russian troops less than two weeks later.

Speaking inside the parliament building, European Commission President Jose Manuel Barroso suggested to reporters he realized the anniversary came amid Hungary's largest political crisis since the collapse of Communism. However, he said he believes the political parties can overcome the difficulties.

"I have great confidence in the democracy in Hungary," said Jose Manuel Barroso. "We have democratic institutions and as I said in my speech in a democracy there is not a single problem for which we cannot find a political solution."

Barosso said he could not agree with the view that the goals of the revolution remain unrealized. He said although the revolt was crushed, it helped create a movement that enabled Europe to eventually be united in peace, freedom and democracy.

In Gyorgy's own words:

"Peter and I had been so looking forward to being involved in this event. How sad that the long-awaited 50th Anniversary of the Uprising should be spoilt by politics, with everyone blaming each other. Perhaps the next Anniversary will be different..."

A disappointed Gyorgy at Corvin Place in October 2006 for the 50th Anniversary of the Hungarian Uprising, showing the photo of him as a young Freedom Fighter on page 112 of *A Brave Nation* by Anna Ambrosy.

THE DEPARTMENT OF
THE PRIME MINISTER AND CABINET

3-6 NATIONAL CIRCUIT
CANBERRA, A.C.T. 2600

TELEPHONE: (02) 6271 5111
FACSIMILE: (02) 6271 5414

1 July 2003

Mr Peter Nadasdy

Dear Mr Nadasdy

Thank you for your correspondence of 19 June 2003 to the Prime Minister enclosing a copy of "A Brave Nation, a short political and social history of 20th Century Hungary" by Anna Ambrosy. I have been asked to reply on Mr Howard's behalf.

The time you have taken to forward the publication is appreciated.

Again, thank you for taking the time to write to Mr Howard.

Yours sincerely

Ministerials Officer
Ministerial Correspondence Unit

Letters from the Australian Prime Minister's Department and 10 Downing Street, thanking Peter Nadasdy for sending copies of *A Brave Nation* by Anna Ambrosy.

10 DOWNING STREET
LONDON SW1A 2AA

From the Direct Communication Unit

8 April 2003

Mr Peter Nadasdy

Australia

Dear Mr Nadasdy

The Prime Minister has asked me to thank you for your recent letter and the book entitled 'A Brave Nation'.

Yours sincerely

MELISSA CHOWDHURY

Closing Remarks

IN 2003 MY brother Peter sent a copy of the book *A Brave Nation* by Anna Ambrosy to Prime Minister Tony Blair in the hope that it might give him a better understanding of events in Hungary in 1956 and afterwards. He received a letter of acknowledgement.

As mentioned in an earlier chapter, my brother was interviewed by Anna Ambrosy in Australia and supplied her with photos of me as a young freedom fighter, which eventually appeared in the book. Sadly, Anna died a few years ago.

It was Peter sending me a signed copy of this book, with a personal message from the author on the flyleaf, that prompted me to tell my own story for the first time. I had shown the book to some of my friends in England at the time but they didn't believe the boy in the photograph was really me. I had to find another photo of me taken soon after I arrived in England in order to convince them!

My friends and work colleagues were also surprised that I had never talked about the events of 1956 until I explained that the memories were so painful that I had tried to blank them from my mind. Reading those books by Anna Ambrosia and Eva Orban had brought memories flooding back and I began to talk about my own experiences.

Eva Orban was a Hungarian writer whose family lived in the same apartment block as my own family in the 1950s, although she was younger than me. Her father owned a small shop on the ground floor that sold groceries. When I had a forint to spare I would buy sweets from him. I would earn this money by shovelling coal for a merchant who ran small business from a cellar beneath our apartment block, during the short time I was allowed home each year from the correctional institution.

Eva's book made me determined to tell my story, which I had kept secret for so many years. Looking back, I realise what a heart-breaking situation it was for my whole family. Peter and I had participated in the Uprising for patriotic reasons, hoping that we could be part of a glorious revolution that would free our country from Russian domination. Unfortunately this did not happen and when the Uprising was crushed we were faced with an agonising choice; leave our country and our family behind and go into exile or stay and face the consequences.

We chose to leave, of course, and both Peter and I were fortunate enough to make new lives for ourselves in our adopted countries of Australia and England. But we had to leave our mother and siblings behind in Hungary, which is something we always regretted. We both wished we could have done more to help them financially and materially but this was difficult since neither of us was able to earn much money in our early years in exile and, besides, Hungary was still under Communist rule, making it impossible to send anything to our family there without it being intercepted by the authorities.

However, I have no doubt that leaving Hungary was the right thing to do because many years later, after returning to Hungary to visit, we discovered that the secret police had come looking for us in the middle of the night at my mother's apartment shortly after we had left the country. My mother was so frightened by this incident that for a while she moved away and lived in Buda, on the other side of the River Danube, until she felt it was safe enough to return to Pest.

Peter also learned that a friend of his who had stayed in Hungary after the revolution was arrested and locked up for 15 years. He didn't live long after being released.

More than a quarter of a century had passed before I felt safe to return to see my family again in 1982. Even then, the authorities were less than welcoming but fortunately the situation has improved in the intervening years. Sylvia and I have returned many times and it feels like a second home even to her now.

For me it has been a dream come true to be able to return to see my Hungarian family. Hungarians are warm and hospitable people and we are always made to feel very welcome. There is even an English pub in Buda called *The John Bull,* with a picture of John Bull on the wall. The landlord asked me if I knew him!

I am still a lorry driver and travel all over the country, making collections and deliveries. At weekends I often visit the Services at nearby Tamworth Industrial Estate to see if there are any Hungarian lorries parked up for the weekend. If there are I stop to chat to the drivers in Hungarian and always ask if there is anything I can do to help them.

On one occasion a driver had a big problem when the cashpoint would not accept his card for some reason and he couldn't buy fuel to get home. I was able to sort the situation out with the salesgirl, who was happy to accept his card after I advised him to show her his driving licence with his signature on it. He was so relieved he said, "I think Jesus sent you to help me!"

Some years ago when in the North of England I stopped for a break and discovered that there was a Hungarian Club in Rochdale. It was like a small working men's club and I went there a few times when I was in the area. It was nice to speak my own language to people there. I told them that I had been in the Uprising and took my photo to show them, which they put on the wall.

Sadly, the club is closed now. The second generation, born in this country, are not interested in this kind of club. It's only to be expected. Like my own children they have grown up here and are English rather than Hungarian. Those events long ago did not affect them personally; for them it's just part of their history.

The Statue of *Pesti Srac* (City Kid) also known as Janchi (Little John), the youngest boy killed during the Uprising.

Below we see Gyorgy's wife Sylvia visiting the monument in 2015.

Appendix 1: The 16 Student Demands

1   We demand the immediate evacuation of all Soviet troops, in conformity with the provisions of the Peace Treaty.

2   We demand the election by secret ballot of all Party members....

3   A new Government must be constituted under the direction of Imre Nagy.[1]

4   We demand public enquiry into the criminal activities of Mihaly Farkas and his accomplices. Matyas Rakosi, who is the person most responsible for crimes of the recent past as well as for our country's ruin, must be returned to Hungary for trial before a people's tribunal.

5   We demand general elections by universal, secret ballot are held throughout the country to elect a new National Assembly, with all political parties participating. We demand that the right of workers to strike be recognised.

6   We demand revision and re-adjustment of Hungarian-Soviet and Hungarian-Yugoslav relations in the fields of politics, economics and cultural affairs, on a basis of complete political and economic equality, and of non-interference in the internal affairs of one by the other.

7   We demand the complete reorganisation of Hungary's economic life under the direction of specialists. The entire economic system... must be re-examined in the light of conditions in Hungary and in the vital interest of the Hungarian people.

8   Our foreign trade agreements and the exact total of reparations that can never be paid must be made public. We demand to be precisely informed of the uranium deposits in our country, on their exploitation and on the concessions to the Russians in this area. We demand that Hungary have the right to sell her uranium freely at world market prices to obtain hard currency.

9   We demand complete revision of the norms operating in industry and an immediate and radical adjustment of salaries in accordance with the just requirements of workers and intellectuals. We demand a minimum living wage for workers.

10 We demand that the system of distribution be organised on a new basis and that agricultural products be utilised in rational manner. We demand equality of treatment for individual farms.

11 We demand reviews by independent tribunals of all political and economic trials as well as the release and rehabilitation of the innocent. We demand the immediate

---

[1] (Nagy became Chairman the Council of Ministers of the People's Republic of Hungary this time by popular demand, during the anti-Soviet revolution. Soon he moved toward a multiparty political system.)

repatriation of prisoners of war (World War 2) and of civilian deportees to the Soviet Union, including prisoners sentenced outside Hungary.

12 We demand complete recognition of freedom of opinion and of expression, of freedom of the press and of radio, as well as the creation of a daily newspaper for the MEFESZ Organisation (Hungarian Federation of University and College Students' Associations).

13 We demand that the statue of Stalin, symbol of Stalinist tyranny and political oppression, be removed as quickly as possible and be replaced by a monument in memory of the martyred freedom fighters of 1848-49.

14 We demand the replacement of emblems foreign to the Hungarian people by the old Hungarian arms of Kossuth. We demand new uniforms for the Army

which conform to our national traditions. We demand that March 15 be declared a national holiday and that the October 6th be a day of national mourning on which schools will be closed.

15 The students of the Technological University of Budapest declare unanimously their solidarity with the workers and students of Warsaw and Poland in their movement towards national independence.

16 The students of the Technological University of Budapest will organise as rapidly as possible local branches of MEFESZ....(The League of Hungarian University and College Student Association)(4)

This printed leaflet listing the 16 demands was circulated prior to the Uprising.

(Source American Hungarian Assoc.)

Appendix 2: Reports from the Federal Council of Hungarian Associations in Australia

"The Hungarian Uprising 1956, as seen by Australian leaders of the time," compiled by Endre Csapa on behalf of the Federal Council of Hungarian Associations in Australia, October 1981, produced by Bulletin Press and News Services, Merrylands, N.S.W.2160 Australia.

Reference pages 3-4, EVENTS LEADING TO THE REFORMIST REVOLUTION, RG Menzies, Prime Minister (30th Oct. 1956, House of Representatives.)

"The revolt in Hungary appears to be a popular protest against Soviet domination... Under the Hungarian peace treaty, executed in February 1947, to which the Soviet Union, the United Kingdom, the United States and the other allied and associated powers were parties, the Soviet Union was required to withdraw her troops from Hungary when Soviet occupation forces had been withdrawn from Austria last year.

Article 2 of the political clauses of the Hungarian peace treaty to which Australia was a party, provided that-

1   Hungary shall take all measures necessary to secure all persons under Hungarian jurisdiction, without discrimination as to race, sex, language or religious worship, of political opinion and of public meeting.

2   Hungary further undertakes that the laws in force in Hungary shall not, either in their content or in their application, discriminate or entail any discrimination between persons of Hungarian nationality on the ground of their race, sex, language or religion, whether in reference to their persons, property, business, professional or financial interests, status, political or civil rights or any other matter.

These provisions were, of course, plainly inserted for the protection of the Hungarian people who had and have a perfect right to require that they should be honoured. It is quite clear that in fact they have, over the years, been substantially disregarded. The Warsaw pact of May 1955, provided for the use of soviet forces to repel foreign aggression against the satellites.

"... A treaty provision does not become a domestic matter simply because the conflicts take place within the boundaries of one nation.

Reference: The Hungarian Uprising 1956, Pages 5-6, and Eugene Gorman, Q.C. (Gorman Report and the Problem of Hungary, 29th March 1957 for The United Nations.)

"Prior to the revolution the standard of living was such that the people had become very embittered.

Food was scarce and expensive and little meat was available...the nation's products went to Russia.

There was an acute housing shortage and the average worker lived in very cramped conditions.

The population lived in an atmosphere of mutual fear and mistrust.

No one dared to criticize the Government either in public of among friends for fear that the Security Police (A.V.H.) or the Communist Party might hear of it. There was a deep-seated resentment against the A.V.H. and the Communist Party because of their continuous investigations of the private lives of the people and their actions, and for sending critics into political prisons of concentration camps.

Hungarian Trade Unions were merely instruments of Government and the Party to communicate and enforce Government instructions and decrees. The unions did nothing to assist of represent the workers, or protect their human rights."

Reference: Page 6, Keith C.O. Shan, (Australian member of the United Nations Special Committee on Hungary. Shann Report, 20th June 1957.)

"In any study of the causes of the uprising, attention is necessarily focussed on the penetration of Hungary by the Soviet influence over a period of years. This influence was felt in the life of every Hungarian citizen. It dictated the foreign language he was to study at School, it obliged Hungary to accept unfavourable trade agreements with the USSR which aversely affected his standard of living, and it maintained, on the Soviet model, the apparatus of a secret police under the shadow of which he lived."

Rererence: pages 6-7. COMMUNIST PARTY POLICE FIRES ON PEACEFUL DEMONSTRATORS.

R. G. Menzies 30th October 1956, Prime Minister of Australia, House of Representatives.

"In the face of rising public opinion, the politburo saw danger to its own position and tried to reverse the trend. Rioting was finally touched off on 23rd October by the action of the police firing into a peaceful demonstration of university students. This was, of course, a violation of the treaty, which guaranteed freedom of political opinion and of public meeting. It quickly developed into a popular uprising...against communism itself, but certainly against Soviet domination.

The Security Council held an emergency meeting on 28th October, on the initiation of the United Kingdom, The United States and France, Australia, also a party to the Hungarian Peace Treaty, was consulted about the course of action and supported this initiation, believing that the United Nations should ventilate and investigate the serious situation that had developed, with a view to preventing further bloodshed.

Of the eleven members of the Security Council, only the Soviet Union voted against discussion of the situation, maintaining that it is a purely domestic affair, an argument the invalidity of which clearly appears from what I have already said to honourable members. The Soviet representative also made clearly false claims that the Western Powers had provoked the rebellion.

The Australian representative on the Security Council expressed, in strong terms, Australia's sympathy with the Hungarian people in their present ordeal, and hoped that the Soviet Union would... leave Hungary to deal with her problems by purely democratic processes... on behalf of the Government... that we welcome any steps which would lead to the establishment of Hungary as a truly independent nation...

Which would guarantee democratic and human rights to her people and would remove any shadow of foreign domination from a people who have made such a notable contribution to the history and culture of a free world."

Reference: THE RISE AND RAPE OF A NATION.

Page 7, Eugene Gorman, Q.C. (Gorman Report on the Problem of Hungary for the United Nations.)

"Russian troops had entered the city before dawn on 24th October. There was heavy fighting in Budapest on 24th and 25th October and on the morning of 25th October a number of people were killed in a demonstration at Parliament Square. Though Russian tanks had fired on the crowd, the fighting in the main was between the people and the A.V.H. The Hungarian Army and the police are stated to have been sympathetic to the people. Russian troops were withdrawn from the city about the end of the month. At this stage, fighting had practically ceased and the people were preparing for a return to work under the Nagy Government. Their hope was an independent Hungary, free from Russian control and completely neutral in its dealings with other nations."

Reference: pages 9-10. THE KADAR GOVERNMENT'S BIRTH OUT OF TANK GUN BARRELS.

On November 4th, the very day the Soviet hordes are killing Hungarians and pulverising Budapest, a declaration is broadcast from the radio at Russian-occupied Szolnok, that Janos Kadar (Hungarian Communist Leader) and Ferenc Munich broke with Prime Minister Imre Nagy, and have set up a Revolutionary Worker-Peasant government because "respected sons of the working class have been exterminated" and this "government" has asked for Soviet help "against fascism and reaction and its murderous bands". This so-called "government's" first step was to piece together a new secret police force. With the help of the Red Army, Kadar established "order" by executions, Bolshevic terror, deportations peoples-courts etc. The Red Army and the Kadar regime are still the pillars of the present "Peoples Republic of Hungary".

Reference: page 10. THE FAILURE OF THE UNITED NATIONS ORGANISATION.

At the time of the brutal Soviet assault on Hungary in 1956, when the whole world witnessed the aggression through the mass media, the United Nations decided to set up a Committee to collect evidence, on what action could be taken. Practically, this decision was the end to hope of any action. All it achieved is a few fine reports made by three Australian Gentlemen; Eugene Gorman, Keith Shann and Dr. Ronald Walker. Australia, as a small power, did its duty. The great powers did nothing but lip service. The Soviet was quick to measure the lack of action from the West.

Reference: pages 10-11. Wilfred Kent Hughes. (Member for Chisholm, 12th September 1957, House of Representatives.)

Soviet authorities have continually flouted every resolution and request by the United Nations with regard to Hungary. The Secretary General and other members… appointed were not allowed to visit Hungary. When a five-man committee was appointed to by the Assembly on 9th January, by a vote of 59 to 8… and permission to visit Hungary was sought, that permission was refused. The Hungarian Government, such as it was, informed the United Nations on 10th January:

No committee of any kind has the right to conduct investigations into the Hungarian question by quoting testimony form unauthorised and biased persons to establish observation in Hungary in order to obtain information.

Since 1956, tragedy has been heaped on tragedy, terror upon terror. All the worst features of the old regime have been restored in even stricter forms. Prison or concentration camps and the Soviet A.V.H. control have been re-established and 50,000 Hungarians…reported to have been sold into slavery…

Reports that arrests and trials without acquittals are still continuing.

Nearly 200,000 sought freedom in other countries by fleeing over the Austrian border. 50,000 Hungarians were killed or wounded, 10,000 of whom lie buried under the rubble of the 8,000 odd buildings that were destroyed. 20,000 flats were damaged.

Is any further evidence needed of the extent and magnitude of the feeling throughout the whole country when those were the casualties, deportees and refugees, in a population of slightly less than 10,000,000?

Reference: page 12. W C Wentworth (Member for Mackellar, 12th September 1957, House of Representatives.)

Our task is to make the evidence known. The report of the United Nations should receive the widest circulation…going into High schools and universities so that the young people should know the facts of life; the young people's movement against tyranny and how people have to live. What has happened in Hungary is surely appalling.

Appendix 3: United Nations Report on 'The problem of Hungary'

Refererence: pages 93-95, A Brave Nation published in 2001, author Anna Ambrosy. The uprising from A. Ambrosy's research.

At the joint request of the United Nations, France and Great Britain, the UN Security Council had already been called into session for a discussion on the Hungarian situation on October 28th, 1956, while the Revolution was still going on.

The United Nations General Assembly established a special committee on the Problem of Hungary for the purpose of investigating the Hungarian 1956 Revolution. Five countries delegated members- Australia, Denmark, Ceylon, Tunisia and Uruguay.

The mandate given to the Special Committee by the United Nations General Assembly was to carry out a full and objective investigation on all aspects of Soviet Intervention in Hungary by armed forces and by other means and on the effects of such intervention on the political development of Hungary. In carrying out this mandate, the Committee studied a rich documentation supplied by Governments and obtained from other sources, while it closely questioned more than a hundred witnesses, representing every stratum of Hungarian society, whose testimony fills 2,000 pages in the verbatim record.

The General Assembly asked that the investigation should be pursued in Hungary also, but the attitude of the (so called) Hungarian Government did not allow the Committee to carry out this part of it's mandate.

The essence of these conclusions is as follows:

(Reference: A Brave Nation published in 2001, author Anna Ambrosy page 96 and United Nations Report, New York, 1957: pages 20-31.)

1. It was a spontaneous national uprising, caused by long standing grievances, including the inferior status of Hungary with regard to the USSR.

2. Students, workers, soldiers and intellectuals, many of them Communists or former Communists, led the uprising. Those who took part in it insisted that democratic socialism should be the basis of the Hungarian political structure, and that the land reform and other social achievements should be safeguarded. It is untrue that reactionary circles in Hungary started the uprising.

3. The uprising was not planned in advance, but actually took participants by surprise. It's timing was connected with Poland's successful move for greater independence from the USSR and the disappointment

caused by the speech of Erno Gero on his return from Yugoslavia on 23rd October, 1956 when it was hoped that he would adopt a sympathetic attitude towards the popular demands voiced on 22nd October by the Hungarian students.

4.   It would appear that the Soviet authorities had taken steps as early as 20th October to make armed intervention possible. Evidence exists on troop movements, from that date on, and Soviet troops from outside Hungary were used even in the first intervention. In Hungary, signs of opposition were evident before 23rd October.

5.   The demonstrations on 23rd October 1956, were at first entirely peaceable, and no evidence has been discovered that any demonstration intended to resort to force. The change was due to the action of the AVH in opening fire on the people outside the Radio Building and the appearance of the Russian soldiers in Budapest as enemies in combat, which further united the people.

6.   Mr Nagy did not issue any invitation to the Soviet authorities to intervene, the first or the second time in November, and the Committee has no evidence as to the circumstances in which an invitation was issues at all. Similar conditions apply to the alleged invitation by Mr. Kadar's government for the Soviet troops to intervene on the second occasion. There is abundant evidence that Soviet preparations for this intervention had been underway since the last days in October 1956.

7.   Mr Nagy was not at first free to exercise the full powers of the Premiership. By the time the grip of the AVH had been loosened, the real power lay with the Revolutionary and Workers Councils. Mr Nagy, seeing that his countrymen were united in the desire for

other forms of Government and for the departure of the Soviet troops, threw in his lot with the insurgents.

8.   During the few days of freedom, the popular nature of the uprising was proved by the appearance of a free press and radio and by general rejoicing among the people. The disbanding of the AVH removed a burden of fear.

9.   A number of lynchings and beatings by the crows concerned, in almost all cases, members of the AVH or those who were believed to have co-operated with them.

10.   Steps taken by the Workers' Council during this period were aimed at giving the workers real control of nationalised undertakings and abolishing unpopular institutions, such as the production norms which were said to make heavy demands on the Hungarian economy for the benefit of the Soviet Union. During the days of freedom, while negotiations continued with the Soviet authorities for the withdrawal of Russian troops, attempts were made to clear up the streets of Budapest and life was beginning to return to normal. The insurgents had agreed to amalgamate, while maintaining their identity, in a National Guard, which would have been responsible, with the Army and Police, for maintaining order.

11.   In contrast to the demands put forward during the uprising for the re-establishment of political rights, basic human rights of the Hungarian people were violated by the Hungarian Governments prior to 23 October, especially up to the autumn of 1955, and that such violations have been resumed since 4 November. The numerous accounts of inhuman treatment and torture by the ÁVH must be accepted as true. Evidence shows that in an attempt to break the revolution,

numbers of Hungarians, including some women, were deported to the Soviet Union and that some may not have been returned to their homes.

12. Since the second Soviet intervention on 4 November, there has been no evidence of popular support for Mr. Kádár's Government. Mr. Kádár has abandoned most of the points made from the revolution progressively, which were promised to the Hungarian people. He has proceeded step by step to destroy the power of the Workers Councils. On the central question of the withdrawal of Soviet troops, he has moved from complete acceptance of the nation's wishes to a refusal to discuss the subject. Capital punishment is applicable to strike activities. The Social Democratic Party has again been forcibly liquidated. General elections have been postponed for two years. Writers and intellectuals are subjected to strong repressive measures. Only a small fraction of the 190,000 Hungarians, mostly young people, who fled the country have accepted his invitation to return.

13. Consideration of the Hungarian question by the United Nations was legally proper and the Treaty of Peace Charter does not justify objections to such consideration. A massive armed intervention by one Power on the territory of another, with the avowed intention of interfering with it's internal affairs must, by the Soviet's own definition of aggression, be a matter of international concern.

Reference: Anna Ambrosy, A Brave Nation, page 157, quoting from Michener, J.A. The Bridge at Andau.

"To conclude, the Revolution in Budapest fell into three parts, which began on October 23rd 1956 and ended on October 29th when the Russians withdrew for tactical reorganisation and practically surrendered the city to the freedom fighters.

The second phase was brief, but extremely sweet. For five days Budapest delighted in the mistaken belief that Hungary was at last free of Russian domination and that some kind of sharply modified communism replace the AVH terror.

The third phase began on November 4th when Russian tanks stormed back into the city in force, imposing a worse terror than the AVH, and horribly crushing the revolution."

Appendix 4: The Start of the Uprising

Reference: The Hungarian Review, "Bloody Thursday, 1956, The Anatomy of the Kossuth Square massacre" published by Gyorgy Granasztoi, author Gabor Jobbagi.

The uprising started in Parliament Square (Orszaghaz ter or Kossuth Square) when thousands of students gathered and a student delegate had peacefully tried to state their demands over the radio.

The students and other Hungarians who were against Communism in the square were fired upon from inside the building, which started the revolution. 60-200 were massacred on Thursday 25th October in the square, known as "Bloody Thursday.

Approximately 20,000 Hungarians died in the two-week conflict and 50,000 were wounded.

"On 25 October 1956 one of the biggest mass murders in Europe in the second half of the 20th century took place on Kossuth Square in front of the Hungarian Parliament building in Budapest."

Witnesses give different accounts of the consequences but many protesters were shot dead and hundreds were injured on 25th October. "The number of dead can be estimated at between 800 and 1,000, including those injured who died later from their wounds."

Student Demonstrations and the origins of Armed Conflict in Budapest

Reference: A Brave Nation by Anna Ambrosy. Pages 106-113

Masses of people and the angry shouting was as a result of various factors arising from the need for freedom from the harsh communist regime: the students had widely spread sixteen political, economic and idealogical points of resolution, typed them, and with the help of office workers, spread them about frantically in Budapest early morning on 23rd October, together with news of supporting a peaceful demonstration. Students requested other universities to join them on 23rd at 10am and work in Budapest stopped. Everyone went out in the streets, read the points and rushed home or to their factories. Every office worker copied these points and spread them. Everyone was talking about it; in conversation, over the telephone so the news spread in a few hours and within a short time Budapest became an ant- hill.

Demonstrations were illegal and this one had been prohibited at 12.53 over the radio, issued by the Minister of the Interior, Laszlo Piros. As the demonstration would no doubt go ahead, Mr. Piros was advised, he stated that he would fire on the demonstrators. This ban was lifted at 2.23pm and announced over the radio. By this time there was an orderly 10,000 people, students, workers, cadets and soldiers.

The 16 points were read out at General Bem's statue by the President of the Writers' Union, Peter Veres and received with great enthusiasm. Most of the crowd proceeded across the Danube to the Parliament Building 1 1/2 kilometres away, joined by people streaming into the centre from all over the city. Radio Free Europe used loudspeakers from a van in the streets to request workers and others to join. By 6pm they were approximately 200,000-300,000 strong.

The intention of the students had been to call everyone they could to join in a peaceful demonstration, meeting at the Embassy of the Polish Peoples Republic and then to have their 16 demands heard over Radio Budapest. This was not allowed so the masses marched to Parliament Square where Former Prime Minister, Mr Imre Nagy, made a disappointing vague, short speech to the crowd asking the peaceful demonstrators to "go quietly home" and leave the Square. His general statement did not calm their mood. Some demonstrators heard the speech from radios placed in open windows, but the majority only heard about it.

Erno Gero's (First Secretary) speech broadcasted at 8pm on 23rd condemned the writers and students 16 demands. He called them "The enemy of the nation and a mob!" This triggered anger by the people who decided to carry out one of the 16 points themselves- to remove the bronze statue of Stalin from the edge of Varosliget, City Park. It was 30 feet high: 9 metres.

Already early in the evening of 23rd October, crowds had assembled around the huge statue of Stalin, from the Bem statue and Parliament Building. Some enthusiastic young people climbed the huge monument to set to work on it. The participants

worked with gusto on it after Gero's speech at 8pm. By 9.30pm the statue fell from its pedestal.

The first shots

Reference: Anna Ambrosy, A Brave Nation, Page 113.

The radio station was the nerve centre of the communist regime in Hungary, housed in a large complex of buildings in Brody Sangor Street near to the museum park. Eighty crack AVH men with machine guns constantly guarded it. The nest of buildings was almost impossible to penetrate without endless permission and security checks. There were two thick wooden doors fortified with oaken beams and studding. The communist leaders of Hungary had long determined that no unruly crowd would ever storm Radio Budapest.

Nevertheless, towards dusk on October 23rd, young people began to gather in the street in front of Radio Budapest. They saw eighty AVH men inside dispose themselves at vantage points and open massive doors for the entrance of large numbers of AVH reinforcements carrying fresh supplies of ammunition. The building would now be twice as difficult to capture.

At 9pm that night, a group of university students arrived at the wooden doors and demanded the right to broadcast to the people of Hungary their demand for certain changes in government policy. It was refused and the students tried to force their way into the building. The crowd observed this defeat and joined the students in trying to push down the doors. The AVH tossed tear-gas bombs into the crowd. Spotlights were flashed onto the crowds who threw stones at the beacons. The AVH fired into the crowd from the building, killing many.

Reference: The American Heritage New Dictionary of Cultural Literacy, Third Edition. Copyright 2005, Houghton Mifflin Co.

As the situation escalated the crowds grew more unruly and attempted to take the station by storm, which is when the first casualties of the Hungarian Revolution fell... The AVH opened fire on the crowd.

This cold-blooded killing provoked a full-scale riot, in which Hungarian soldiers sided with the people against the AVH. Police cars were set on fire, weapons were seized and Communist symbols were torn down and vandalised. That night Erno Gero called on military intervention from the Soviet Union to suppress the uprising.

Hostilities, casualties and damage on 4th November 1956

Reference: UNITED NATIONS REPORT OF THE SPECIAL COMMITTEE ON THE PROBLEM OF HUNGARY New York. 1957. Chapter XVI OTHER VIOLATIONS OF HUMAN RIGHTS AND FUNDAMENTAL FREEDOMS pages 231-232

B. Hostilities during the second intervention by the Soviets on 4th November.

746. ... for the purpose of crushing the Revolution, Soviet tanks moved along the streets of Hungarian towns shooting indiscriminately at armed groups or individuals and at every building from which they believed they were being attacked. In addition to military operations of this kind, there are numerous instances of mortar fire across the Danube from Pest to Buda on inhabited quarters, of artillery fire on buildings from which there was no return fire and of haphazard shooting at defenceless passers-by. It was reported that

twenty to thirty tanks went up and down one Budapest street for about an hour, firing at the buildings until they were completely destroyed. Another incident was: "On 4 November ten armoured cars came towards our positions at Széna Square by way of the Margit Bridge over the Danube. Their guns were pointed at each side of the street in turn. For one and a half kilometres they fired at each house, destroying a large number and killing many people, including women and children. When they arrived at Széna Square they fired at everything within a radius of one kilometre for several hours, although their fire was not returned."

747. Many witnesses have seen Soviet soldiers shot at queues outside bakeries or other food shops. The victims were women and children. Other incidents that aroused indignation were the many cases of shooting at ambulances, Red Cross vehicles and the doctors and nurses in those vehicles.

748. Especially after 4 November, Soviet orders were to crush all resistance by every means that would prove effective. A report to the Budapest City Council stated that "the number of partially or completely destroyed dwellings at 40,000 appears to be exaggerated, and a figure of 20,000 appears nearer to reality." On 1 February, the official Central Statistical Office reported that about 20,000 flats were damaged in Budapest, which represents 4.1 per cent of the total number of flats in the capital. Some 2,217 were completely destroyed. About 260 million forints were needed for reconstruction of these flats.

749. Doctors, nurses and hospital staff complained of having been prevented by Soviet gunfire from assisting the wounded in the streets of Budapest. They did not conceal their indignation in recalling certain cases where Soviet soldiers had entered

hospitals and carried off wounded persons whom they suspected of being "freedom fighters".

750. Witnesses also complained of the improper use of the Red Cross emblem by the ÁVH and the Soviet Army, the lack of respect for the white flag and hands raised in token of surrender. One incident reported related to young boys of thirteen or fourteen years of age who, on meeting Soviet tanks, tore up their shirts to make white flags - a gesture that did not have any effect on the soldiers determined to massacre them. During the first days of the Revolution, many cases were reported where weapons were transported by the ÁVH in ambulances and other vehicles marked with the Red Cross.

751. With regard to the dispatch of medical supplies and of assistance from other countries, the information that the Committee was able to collect does not enable it to arrive at any definite conclusions. Some of the supplies reached their destination and were welcomed with the greatest satisfaction by the medical corps. Later, when the airports were surrounded by Soviet troops and the frontiers closed, the delivery of these medical supplies was delayed.

Award winning sculpture commemorating the 1956 Uprising completed in City Park Budapest in 2006.

Appendix 5: Deportations

Reference: UNITED NATIONS REPORT OF THE SPECIAL COMMITTEE ON THE PROBLEM OF HUNGARY, GENERAL ASSEMBLY, OFFICIAL RECORDS: ELEVENTH SESSION

SUPPLEMENT No. 18 (A/3592) New York. 1957 Page 220 Chapter XV

DEPORTATIONS

Introduction

717. On 3 December, Western correspondents reported that, in the course of an interview in Budapest, István Szirmai, Chief of the Hungarian Government Press Department, had admitted "there were isolated cases in the first days of chaos after 4 November when the Russian authorities arrested and deported young people...

718. On 16 November, the Debrecen paper, Napló, published an article stating that public opinion had been agitated by the news that people were being carried through Debrecen in closed wagons towards Záhony, on the Russian frontier. It added that it had been announced "officially" that such occurrences would not take place in the future and that measures had been taken for the immediate return of the wagons in question...

719. Leaflets were circulated in Budapest containing what purported to be accounts of deportations. One such publication entitled Magyar Október (Hungarian October) dated 15 November 1956 declared that people living near the Western Railway Station in Budapest could hear hammering on the freight cars and that freedom fighters who escaped said that hundreds of captured fighters had been packed into freight cars. Near the Soviet frontier, a wallet was said to have been thrown from a train bound for the USSR. The wallet was alleged to have contained a list of names of Budapest youths who were being deported to the Soviet Union.

Investigation by the Committee

721. The Committee also heard a number of witnesses who had been placed in deportation trains or trucks moving towards the Hungarian-Soviet frontier, but who had been liberated by Hungarian railway workers or freedom fighters. Other witnesses had participated in such liberation activities, and described how they had stopped trains or trucks and freed the prisoners.

722 The Committee subjected all these witnesses to searching cross-examination. As a result of its study of their testimony, and other evidence confirming it, it reached the conclusion that, beyond doubt, deportations to the USSR had indeed taken place, and had taken place in considerable numbers. It was satisfied that the

circumstances in which these deportations had occurred were, in general, as described by the witnesses. The official statements denying that any deportations had occurred in Hungary are therefore not in accordance with the facts. These deportations may be regarded as an effort to undermine potential opposition within Hungary.

C. Seizure of deportees

723. According to the evidence, deportations of Hungarian citizens to the Soviet Union began in the period following the second armed intervention by Soviet forces. The number of such deportations appears to have been particularly large during the three weeks following 4 November. Witnesses said that, on some days, in the middle of November, several trainloads of deportees left Budapest. Deportation trains are said to have arrived in Russia as late as mid December, and some Hungarians are alleged to have been deported even in January 1957. The largest number of deportees seems to have come from the provinces, especially from the eastern part of Hungary. Witnesses testified that they had seen deportees in Soviet prisons from such towns as Karcag, Szombathely, Győr, Kecskemét, Miskolc, Debrecen, Nyíregyháza and Veszprém.

724. In Budapest itself, most of the early arrests were made in a haphazard manner. People were rounded up in the streets in groups that ran into hundreds and sometimes included elderly people and children. According to witnesses, the general practice was to close off part of a street by stationing a tank at each end. Anyone found within the area was taken away. One case was reported where fifty people were liberated from a number of trucks, after which the Russian soldiers immediately arrested fifty other people in their place. (4) Some people were seized in centres of resistance, such as the revolutionary barracks taken over by Soviet troops. Others were taken in house-to-house searches by teams of Russian soldiers and former ÁVH agents, after the fighting had subsided. In the provinces, few were arrested in the streets, but large groups of students, workers or freedom fighters were sometimes arrested together. In some cases, the entire Revolutionary Council in a town or the whole Workers' Council in a factory would be seized.

725. The prisoners were collected in trucks or Soviet armoured cars and generally taken to political prisons or to other assembly places. Witnesses described how, in Budapest, groups of 400-500 people were assembled in underground halls at the Eastern and Western Railway Stations. On 6 November, according to a witness, ninety men and eight women were kept in a Budapest church for three days before being taken to a deportation train. Some prisoners were held captive in the military barracks, such as the Kilián and Petőfi Barracks in Budapest, and then transported to Vecsés, a railway station south-east of Budapest. Prisoners were searched for weapons, questioned and any valuables or papers in their possession were confiscated. In some cases, it appeared that their shoes and top clothing were taken away. Sometimes, prisoners remained at the places of detention up to four days or longer, after which they were taken to heavily guarded trains or trucks.

726. Most of the trains bearing deportees to the Soviet Union went through Záhony, the frontier station between Hungary and the Soviet Union, but deportation trains are also reported to have crossed into Romania. The Committee, however, has no conclusive proof that any Hungarians were taken to Romania, apart from those who

accompanied Mr. Nagy.(5) Trains bound for the USSR took either the Cegléd-Szolnok-Debrecen Nyíregyháza line, or that through Gödöllö-Hatvan Miskolc. Witnesses testified that these trains consisted of sealed freight cars or cattle trucks. There were usually from 20 to 35 wagons on each train, although sometimes there were less. These trains carried nothing but deportees, from 30 to 70 in each wagon. During the journey, the captives received scant supplies of food and there were no adequate sanitary facilities. Men and women all travelled together. Each wagon was guarded by Soviet troops and the engine-drivers were Russian.(6)

727. Many of the prisoners threw from the trains hastily-scribbled notes appealing for help and giving their names and addresses, so that their families could be notified. These messages were picked up by railway workers and other Hungarians, who arranged that as many as possible reached their destinations. One witness told the Committee that, out of seventeen messages thrown out of a train by himself, no fewer than eight reached his family.

728. Another witness reported that he, together with eight others, had been taken to the Soviet Union from the city jail at Nyíregyháza, near the Russian border, in two Russian Red Cross cars. In one case a witness stated that the deportees were forced to travel, in bitterly cold weather, without coats in open trucks.

729. When the freedom fighters stopped a deportation train, by removing the rails or by setting the signals, heavy fighting usually took place before the captives were liberated. In one case, however, the Russian guards fled without fighting. One of these liberation exploits took place while the train was still in a Budapest station, while the Committee also heard reports of the liberation of deportees close to the Russian and Romanian frontiers.

730. Most of the deportees were captured by Soviet troops, but some were seized by former members of the ÁVH. Some witnesses stated that, while being held in Hungary, they had been physically maltreated on a few occasions by Russian soldiers, but particularly by members of the ÁVH. Some were submitted to lengthy interrogation by ÁVH agents during which they received harsh and inhuman treatment. One witness reported that, before being taken to the USSR, he had been beaten by an ÁVH officer, until he signed a confession that he was a counter-revolutionary. Those who were found to be carrying arms were beaten; often they were not given food and were threatened with execution. In some cases, pretence was made that execution was imminent. One witness was placed against a wall by soldiers, who then fired all round him. Witnesses testified about several cases in which women were abused. The soldiers told one witness that he would be sent to forced labour in the USSR, while others were told that they would be sent to Siberia. It is noteworthy that witnesses stated that, with a few exceptions, they had been much better treated by Soviet officers and soldiers after they arrived in the USSR, where there were fewer troops of Mongolian origin.

D. Experience of deportees in the USSR

731. ...more deportees arrived from Hungary. It was estimated that the prison, after it was filled up, held at least 2,000 persons, all of whom were believed to be Hungarian ... the first of whom (deportees) seem to have arrived on 7 November. One witness said that it was already crowded by 10 November. One said that forty-two people were confined in a room large enough for about

fourteen and one witness was locked in a room with other people, in which there was not enough space to lie down..., Uzgorod was a place of assembly, and trains carrying deportees went further eastwards, while more deportees arrived from Hungary. It was estimated that the prison, after it was filled up, held at least 2,000 persons, all of whom were believed to be Hungarian.

734. There were women among the prisoners. The majority of deportees were young people, many of them not more than sixteen and some even younger. There were also some elderly persons, one a sixty-two-year-old farmer, who did not know why he had been deported, and another, a sixty-seven-year-old leader of the Independent Smallholders' Party. The majority of the deportees in the prison seem to have been soldiers or freedom fighters.

Stalin's empty boots are all that remains of the statue that once stood in Budapest and now serve as a poignant reminder of the years of Soviet Communist oppression in Hungary and of the Uprising in 1956 that dared to challenge it.

Appendix 6: The Welcome Refugees

Reference: 10th February 2015. The Welcome Refugees, Paul Nemes 1999

Hungarians began to leave their country in large numbers once it became obvious that the Soviet Union was not willing to accept Hungarian neutrality and when it became clear that the West would not risk the current status quo - the cornerstone of East-West relations - for the sake of a small Central European country. Already on 28 October, the Austrian Foreign Ministry sent the following message to London, Paris and Washington: "To all appearances, the uprising in Hungary will come to an end following massive Soviet military intervention. In that event, it can be presumed that larger Hungarian armed formations will cross into Austria." (Ferenc Cseresnyes, "The '56 Exodus to Austria", The Hungarian Quarterly, Vol 40, No 154, 1999).

Most Hungarians disposed of their weapons shortly before crossing into Austria, but the Austrians were correct in assuming that a large number would leave.

On 4 November, the Soviet armoured attack on Budapest and other major Hungarian cities began. By noon, five thousand Hungarians had already crossed the Austrian border. In total, more than 200,000 people left Hungary after the failed Uprising. Just as they had fought in hope of a US and Western military intervention, Hungarians left for a life in the West they had heard so much about on Radio Free Europe and Voice of America. Although a transit country, it was Austria - a neutral country with no capacity to help Hungary militarily or otherwise - that was the least hesitant to accept Hungarian refugees.

The politics of guilt

The West's lack of action left governments with a feeling of guilt. Therefore, Hungarian refugees were welcomed with open arms.

The West and the UN mobilised on a grand scale to assist the flood of refugees. Countries rushed to take the displaced Hungarians. As the situation in Austria became almost unmanageable between 7 and 14 November, seven countries offered to take Hungarians refugees.

Further Reading

A Brave Nation: *A Short Political and Social History of 20th Century Hungary* by Anna Ambrosy, Hungarian Life Publishing, Australia 2001.

Amit '56-rol mindenkinik tudia kell (The Truth About '56) by Eva Orban, Pro Patria, Budapest 2006.

Cry Hungary: *Uprising 1956* by Reg Gadney, Atheneum, 1986.

Esemenyei 1956 terkepen es kepeken *(What happened in 1956 map and pictures)* written/edited by Horvath Miklos, Marton Matyas & Mosonyi Laszlo, published by Honvedelmi Miniszterium Terkepeszeti Kozhasznu Tarsasag, Budapest 2006.

Hungarian Revolution 1956 by Erwin A. Schmidl & László Ritter, Osprey 2006.

Igazságot '56-nak! (True '56 History) Parts 1, 2 & 3 by Éva Orbán, Pro Patria, Budapest 2011.

One Day That Shook the Communist World: *The 1956 Hungarian Uprising and Its Legacy* by Paul Lendvai, Princeton University Press, 2008

The Unexpected Revolution: *Social Forces in the Hungarian Uprising* by Paul Kecskemeti, Stanford University Press, 1961.

Thirteen Days That Shook the Kremlin by Tibor Meray, Howard L. Katzander, Praeger, 1959.

Twelve Days: *The Story of the 1956 Hungarian Revolution* by Victor Sebestyen, Vintage Books USA, 2007.

Uprising: *The Hungarian Revolution of 1956.* David Irving, Focal Point Publications, 1981.